The Automotive Service Manager's Bible

*Fundamentals and Best Practices
for Improving Service Department Profitability*

Charlie Waters

The Automotive Service Manager's Bible
Fundamentals and Best Practices
for Improving Service Department Profitability

Published by Spines Publishing Platform
Isbn:979-8-89569-894-5

The Automotive Service Manager's Bible

*Fundamentals and Best Practices
for Improving Service Department Profitability*

CHARLIE WATERS

*This book is dedicated to my incredible wife, Chris,
and my amazing daughter, Maezie.
Thank you both for being my guiding light.*

CONTENTS

INTRODUCTION

"In the beginning God created the heavens and the earth" (Genesis 1:1).If this book is going to be called the "Bible", it is only appropriate to begin the preface with the first verse of the bible. The title of this book is "The Automotive Service Manager's Bible". Please do not be offended by the term Bible in the title, as dictionary.com defines the term bible as: "any book, reference work, periodical, etc., accepted as authoritative, informative, or reliable." I believe the real "Bible" to be not only a history book, but a psychology book of knowledge, character, respect and wisdom. As it relates to operating a dealership service department, I trust that this book will do a bit of the same.

Let the Story Begin

Many, many years ago, man developed a carriage pulled by one or more horses. It was a great alternative to walking or riding a bicycle, as it allowed multiple passengers to move from point A to point B, using the efforts of one or two horses, as well as the transportation of goods that could not be moved by humans alone.

By 1900, it is estimated that there were 24 million horses "working" in North America. This included personal carriages, taxis, and plow horses. Each horse would generate between 20 and 50 pounds of manure each day. In New York City alone, it was estimated that the 100,000 horses generated 2.5 million pounds of waste each day, not to mention the gases emitted and the disposal of dead horses. This was certainly not sustainable! The answer to this pollution was the internal combustion engine and the horseless carriage, or automobile. Fast forward to the 21st century. As the popularity of the automobile has grown to become essential to most families, the service department's challenges have grown as well.

1. Better-built vehicles that require very little maintenance and repair. This is constantly getting worse, or better, depending on whose perspective you're looking from, consumer or repair facility! This includes EV vehicles that require nearly zero maintenance.

2. Technological advancements require a technician to wear many hats, from a plumber to an electrician and from an engineer to a laborer.

3. A deteriorating workforce is caused by the aging of technicians and a perceived lack-of-interest in this field by the younger generation entering a more competitive workforce that demands higher and more consistent wages.

4. Customer demands "perfection" in work quality and convenience.

5. The desire, by many of us, to do things the way that we have always done them, despite the huge changes in society and technology, is the definition of insanity! Let's face it: most service managers are following in the footsteps of their previous manager, who either got fired or quit because they couldn't take the intense pressure or deal with change anymore!

A former Big Three executive that I had come to know enjoyed telling the story of riding a mechanical bull. His story painted a picture of the average service manager that comes to work each day with great intentions (conducting employee reviews, building and training a new process, etc.), then he or she climbs on the mechanical bull, flips the switch, and says: "Open the doors." The next thing you know, it's 5 or 6:00 p.m., and he or she turns off the bull and says: "WOW! What a day! I'll see y'all tomorrow."

A great friend of mine describes this as: "If you don't have a plan for the day, the day has a plan for you."

The term for this scenario is: "Consumed by Current Reality". The manager spends their day reacting to events rather than managing them. As a result, they find minimal time to implement improvements or monitor the progress, or lack of progress, that the changes have made. So, get off the bull! Successful businessmen and businesswomen have to create a simplified approach to managing their businesses.

A friend of mine worked for the same dealership for approximately 30 years. He began his career as a technician. After about 5 years, he decided to throw his hat in at becoming a Service Advisor. A couple of years of service advisor, then a couple of years of new car prep manager (this was the days when the dealership installed stereos, leather seats and air conditioners). After about 10 total years, my friend was promoted to Assistant Service Manager. His role was to manage and assist the advisors with the retail and fleet customers, provide technical assistance for the technicians and whatever else the day demanded (ride the bull). The Service Director handled most everything else (warranty, payroll, expenses, etc.).

After working in the assistant manager position for about five years, one Monday afternoon, the General Manager (GM) called him to his office. The GM informed him that, at the end of the day, he was going to terminate his boss (the Service Director) and that he, the assistant, was going to replace him. (Bittersweet!) My friend continued his employment at the same dealership for another fifteen years.

The Challenges:

1. His boss was also his friend. While his soon-to-be ex-boss had a lot of personal issues, he knew that his friendship with him was about to end. But he also understood that there were performance issues that were causing his termination.

2. Almost everything that he knew about being a Service Manager was learned from a person who is getting fired today! For him to continue the same practices and expect better results would be insanity.

My friend was me. Fortunately, or unfortunately, this is a similar situation that many of us managers have gone through. After my first few nights without sleep, on advice from a friend and mentor, a Service Manager at another dealership, I grabbed a legal pad and made a list of every duty that I was responsible for and every duty that the previous Service Director was responsible for. I, quickly, became the hardest working Service Director on the planet (so, it seemed)! I worked seven days a week…rode the bull 5-6 of them days! Failure was not an option! Two and a half years later, the business was doing good, but it was wearing me out. I became the scapegoat for every customer that had been worn thin by the "system."

Recognizing that, my dealer had crossed paths with a consultant, whose name is Greg. Greg became my next mentor. Greg was extremely knowledgeable of the "art" of simplifying the service business. He taught me many of the fundamentals and concepts that I will be covering in this book. More than 30 years later, we remain great friends. Many ideas discussed in this book were developed around Greg's ideas and concepts.

While Greg and many others have been positive mentors or influencers, I've also learned that not all of the mentors in life are necessarily positive influences. Instead, sometimes we can be positively influenced by other's mistakes or misbehavior, as long as we have the ability to recognize this behavior as a mistake. It turns out that my early Service Director displayed an abundance of misbehavior.

The **AUTOMOTIVE SERVICE MANAGER'S BIBLE** is designed to assist Service Managers and Directors in overcoming some of these challenges and mistakes that others have made. Like all businesses, the automotive service business is quite simple once we learn to stop complicating it. Remember, there's only one way to eat an elephant: "One bite at a time."

Chapter One is a conversation about **culture.** Culture is the amazing spirit that drives the attitude and vision of how our dealership and service department perform.

Chapter Two turns to: "Managing the Chaos". This is a discussion of two management techniques that will assist you in understanding the pros and cons of every process that you plan to implement. This can be the secret to getting off of "the bull". As you review these techniques, please consider that **NO CHANGE** is sustainable without management follow-up. It is important that you build your vision to balance the two techniques that you and your staff can effectively manage.

Chapter Three – The Flat Rate Mentality. This is a study of what causes many technicians to behave the way they do and the things we can do to address these challenges.

Chapters Four through Eight: The Fundamentals of Service Department Profitability. It is **not possible** to improve service department profitability without changing one or more of these fundamentals! In each chapter, we discuss in detail, along with thoughts, tips, and ideas for improvement.

Chapter Nine is a discussion of using benchmarks and the pro forma to reverse engineer your business for success. Once you have created your base pro forma, you can calculate where you need to be and back into the changes that can improve your current situation.

Chapter Ten is a summary and discussion of "Building a Playbook". Every manager should have a notebook or electronic folder with documents of every process that they expect to implement. A good friend and mentor of mine always said: "If it ain't in writing, it never happened". When you decide to change a process: a) solicit input; b) document and write the final process; c) train the process; and then d) counsel on the process, as needed (use the document).

Chapter Eleven is a discussion of alternatives in shop structures. This chapter discusses the popular structures, the benefits, and the roadblocks to each of these. Please be careful when planning structure changes. The success depends on the input and involvement of your team.

Chapter Twelve is Technician Pay Plans. In today's world, where it is estimated that there is a 600,000+ shortage of technicians, many dealerships are looking to implement different types of technician pay plans as alternates or supplements to flat-rate.

Please note: Several process improvement suggestions are repeated in different sections of this book. This is designed to assist the reader (you, the manager) in understanding the possible options. We trust that this book will be, not only a good read but a good future reference for future considerations. We have built an index in the back of the book to assist you in referencing specific information in the future.

While the suggestions, concepts, and processes are possibilities that may or may not be applicable in your situation and dealership. When implemented properly, in the right situation, and managed properly, these suggestions have proven to work very well in many dealerships. Unless you are extremely comfortable with the implementation of some of these concepts, we highly recommend that you seek advice from a professional service trainer or consultant.

> *"Perfection is not attainable, but if we chase perfection, we can catch excellence."*
>
> ***Vince Lombardi***

CHAPTER 1:
Fixed Operation Culture

While we will discuss many opportunities for process improvement, culture is the guiding light to your department's success. When you operate a department with leadership, honesty, trust, respect, and transparency, a great culture will follow.

What is Culture?"Culture" may be best defined as:

The **Character** of the business

The living, breathing essence of what an organization values, believes, thinks, says, and does. Culture isn't one thing; its everything. Culture is not one person; its everyone. Every day, everyone in your organization contributes to your culture by what they value, believe, think, say, and do.

Culture refers to the shared values, beliefs, and behaviors of an organization, and it influences how employees interact with one another, how decisions are made, and how work is done. Culture plays a critical role in designing an organization's structure and processes. In turn, an organization's structure and processes play an important role in the organization's culture. In this book, you will read a lot about creating written processes to ensure consistency. Without these processes, we are suggesting to our staff that they design and conduct their own individual processes. This is likely to cause huge inconsistencies. The route that you choose becomes a part of your culture.

Every dealership has a culture. Every department has a culture. Hopefully, these cultures mostly align, but you are responsible for your team's culture. Do you want to solve a misunderstanding or win an argument? If you need to win an argument, your people will follow your lead. What does that mean for your customers? For your employees? These are culture questions.

Own your Culture! –Understand your personal strengths and weaknesses. I have been blessed by the good fortune of having worked with and mentored several different people who have turned out to be very successful in their personal management careers. None of these folks were exactly like me (thank goodness), or just like one another. The common denominator is how much they care about their team. How they express this is very unique to each of them. We must use our strengths to lead our team and look for people who complement us. For example, if your personality is one that is focused on relationships and people skills but lacks the discipline of structure, surround yourself with someone whose personality easily performs these disciplines. And, most of all, encourage all of our team members to succeed.

Many dealerships have mission statements. This mission statement should be a summary of the desired results of all, or many, of the stated visions. The management team must own these visions. In addition, you could have an additional mission statement for your department.

Culture must come from the top! It begins with a vision. As a Service Manager, your team must share a vision with the entire dealership. So, what is the vision?

- Dealership and service department reputation in the community.

- Genuine care and concern for the customer - Communication

- Quality of product – Training and skills

- Dealership/department focus on care for associates?

- Profitability of the department and dealership.

- Interaction and understanding between departments.

As a successful Service Manager, you must develop your service department culture by creating your set of standards. These standards involve:

- Key focuses for department.

- Accountability

- Production

- Environmental

A Culture of Accountability

A business with a great culture must have accountability. Cultures of unaccountability occur when accountability is loosely defined or not defined at all by management. Symptoms of unaccountability include statements like:

- It's not my job.

- Finger pointing

- I never understood that.

A culture of accountability must include the following:

- A clear definition of expectations: Playbook documents are created and trained to define most processes.

- Train the team to follow the process – encourage feedback

- Measure Results: **Chapter 2**

- Evaluate success, celebrate good decisions, and coach the bad.

A culture of accountability requires that management empowers their team **with confidence**. As a manager, you must have confidence in your job, position, and standing before you can have confidence in your team members. You must not fear your job; in fact, you should always be thinking of a succession plan, whether it be two, ten, or twenty years from now. This encourages you to fully develop your team.

A culture of accountability requires that management has a willingness to stand up for your team members' decisions. This earns trust; plus, as a manager, you need to accept the fact that everything is your fault. Only when you accept that you own all of the mistakes can you ask everyone to accept their part of the responsibility. If they must point fingers, ask them to point them at you!

A Production Culture

The most important thing that we do in a service department is to produce labor. Without labor, we don't sell parts, hire support staff, satisfy customers, or make any money. Therefore, production should be the most important item of discussion.

In the parts side of the business, we bring in parts inventory that has previously sold or is likely to sell. We place this inventory on the shelves of our warehouse until it sells. In the event the part doesn't sell within a determined period of time, we either return it to the manufacturer or use alternative means to dispose of the obsolete inventory.

Unlike parts, labor inventory has no shelf life. We begin each day with a supply of technician's work hours times productivity. If we do not sell or use these hours, they are gone forever! In our culture **everyone** should be aware of this. Any time that anyone delays this process (parts delays, approvals, special tools, etc.), we lose inventory that we can never recover. A Production Culture minimizes the amount of wasted time. All parties involved in a production culture must do their part to constantly reduce wasted labor time. Possibilities:

- Advisors – Write up quality, approvals, etc.

- Parts Dept. – Parts availability, pre-pulled, pick tickets, etc.

- Dispatch skill match, preloaded shop, etc.

- Porters – Assistance in staging vehicles, parts delivery, etc.

- Management: paying attention to concerns and implementing processes for improvement, measuring production daily.

- Technicians focus on accomplishing goals and providing feedback on roadblocks.

Environmental Culture

Several years ago, we built a brand-new, beautiful, state-of-the-art dealership. We moved from a facility that was over 60 years old. People would swear that the floors were made of dirt. While that wasn't true, it was a concrete floor with 60 years of grease, grime, and wear and tear. In the corners and against the walls were collections of obsolete equipment, broken tools, and spare parts. As we moved into our new facility, employees quickly attempted to duplicate their old environment. This was their comfort zone. We had to quickly institute policy to change the culture before it was too late. While it is never really "too late," it is always easier to be proactive. To this day, this shop is kept immaculately clean. This became the new culture.

- Below is a photo taken at another dealership. As we think about environmental culture, ask yourself the following questions:

- What do you think a technician from this dealership would look like?

- Do you believe the staff in this service department operates with a high level of accountability and pride?

- Would you think that this dealership has the latest in equipment and tool technology that makes this the place to work for technicians?

- Would you like this service department to work on your new $80,000 vehicle?

According to a recent WrenchWay survey (2023), 97% of technicians believe that proper equipment is important, and 82% consider proper equipment to be extremely important. Think of well-maintained, updated equipment and special tools as a part of your culture. A production/environmental-focused culture must consider the availability of quality equipment for your team.

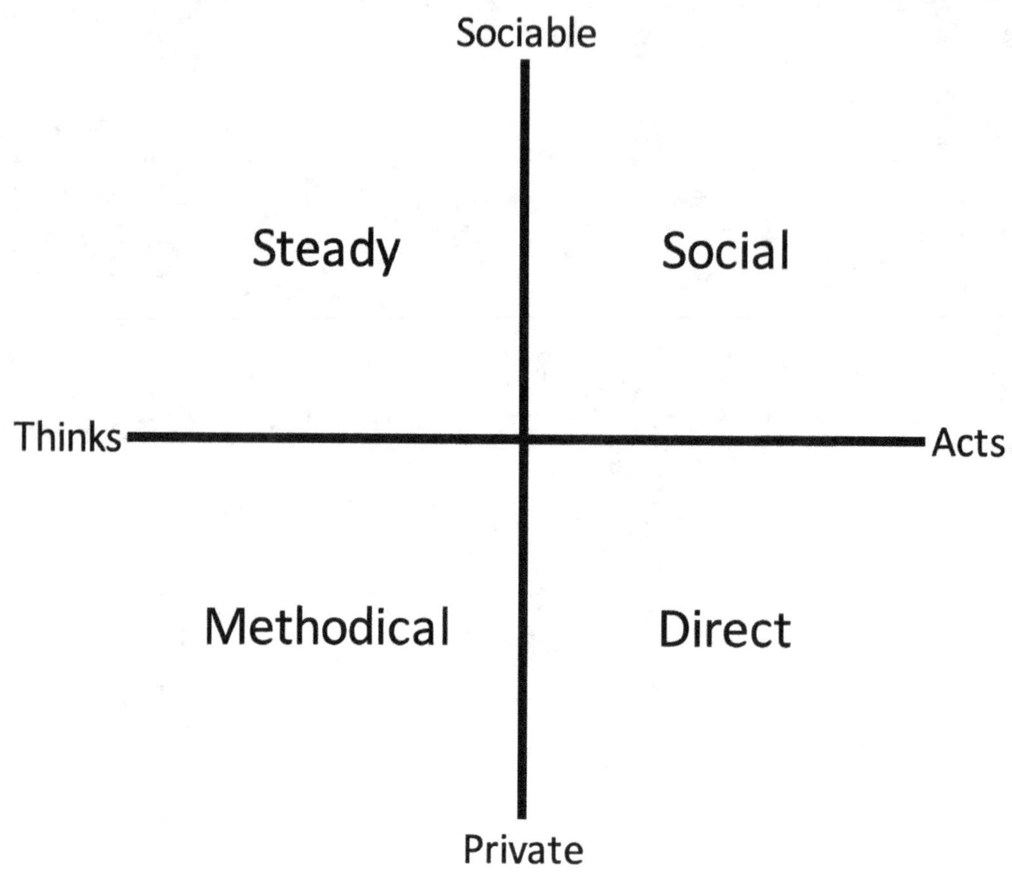

Implementing a Great Culture

Understanding and intertwining different personalities and behavior patterns can be very effective in culture. Different companies call it different things, but essentially, there are four behavior quadrants:

- Direct: "fast-paced," "to the point".

- Social: fast-paced, loves to socialize.

- Steady: sociable, slower-paced, reliable.

- Methodical: analytical, slower-paced, focused on accuracy.

While we all may have a bit of each of these styles, we have a primary style that drives us. For example, many service managers in large dealerships develop into a "Direct" style. This is due to the number of decisions that come at them each day. Many parts managers tend to be the "Methodical" style, as accuracy is critical in the parts department. As a result, a parts manager might see a service manager as being "aloof" or "reckless". And a service manager might see a parts manager as in "slow motion" or suffering from "analysis paralysis". Social style typically makes a good service advisor, if kept under watch, and "Steady" style makes good staff and technicians. A good blend of behavior styles is a good fit for a good culture, as long as we realize the importance of the blend. If you, as a service manager, are a high "Direct" you may want to delegate some of your tedious responsibilities to a "Steady" type or a "Methodical" type. There are several tools available to assist you in further understanding behavior styles, including DiSC and Predictive Index.

Culture should be discussed at every opportunity. The dealership that discusses the customer experience regularly tends to improve the customer experience. The service department that has a production culture tends to have higher productivity due to the enhanced focus.

Organizational Cultures

In addition to Personal Behavior Styles, businesses tend to have Organizational Cultures. In most, for profit, businesses there are four main culture styles. Very much like the Personal Behavior styles, most businesses are not entirely one of the four, rather a primary and probably a secondary style will dominate their overall organizational culture. The most successful companies are likely to possess some form of all of these styles in their overall cultures. There are pros and cons to each, so it is important to have variations. The culture types are:

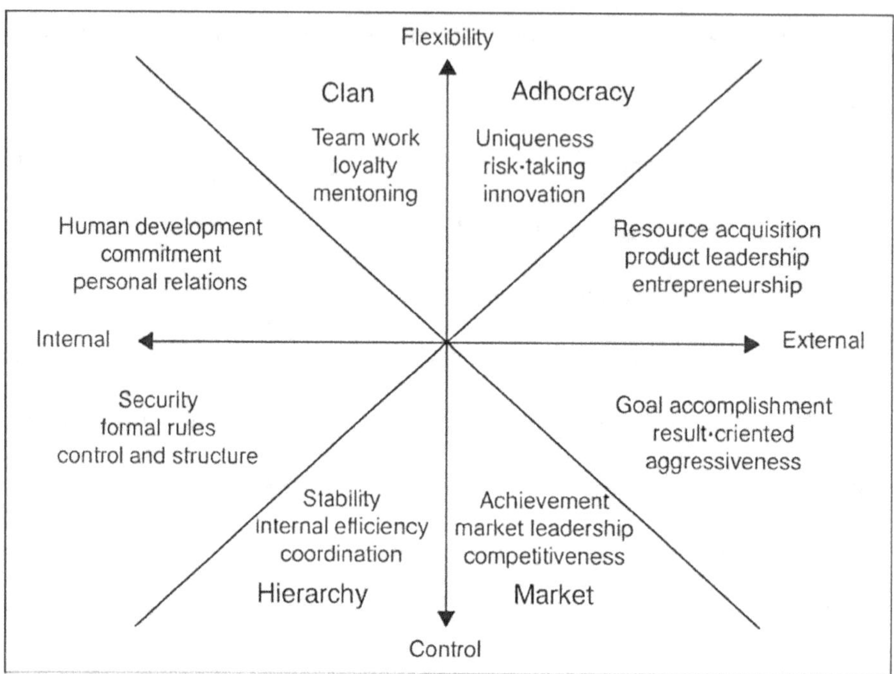

- Clan Culture – The family atmosphere. Great feeling of being a part of things and all are involved in decision making processes that are related to their job. Ever layer of management is approachable and supportive. Managers are considered mentors. Many small businesses operate as their primary style, very effectively.

DANGER: As business grows, lack-of-authority can become a big issue. Associates may overstep their boundaries, believing there are no boundaries. If left unchecked, undisciplined or unbalanced, business could turn into a "banana republic"!

- Adhocracy Culture – Fast paced, take risks, innovative and aggressive. Encourages team to be creative, risk taking; encourages entrepreneurship. Always looking for ways to change and improve. High level of trust.

DANGER: Some associates get dizzy with the pace of change. With change come mistakes, management must be coaches to assure that everyone stays engaged and use mistakes as opportunities for improvement.

- Market Culture – Total focus on market and results. Encourages team to be innovated and often is driven to achieve market dominance. Fast-pace, and high productivity are expected.

  DANGER: High pressure work environment can cause fatigue. The focus on external results can result in neglecting internal processes.

- Hierarchy Culture – Top-down leadership creating strict levels of authority and control. This military style culture emphasizes long-term stability by creating a very clear, structured environment. Associates must always follow the chain-of-command. Designed to cultivate years of steady output.

  DANGER: Slow moving due to bureaucratic nature. Vulnerable to fast-moving smaller companies. Reduced innovation due to rigid structure.

As mentioned before, it is likely that successful companies employe bits of each style in their overall culture. Examples:

- Clan Culture can be very desirable to maintain a positive work environment.

- Adhocracy Culture can be really good for building an innovative team.

- Market Culture can be a great focus on "keeping your eye on the ball" or competition, always looking for a competitive advantage.

- Hierarchy Culture maintains a great focus on accuracy, consistency and chain of command.

The Tale of Two Cultures (a semi-true story)

Once upon a time, there were two extremely successful Fixed Operations Directors. They both had built huge service businesses, with long-tenured, happy employees. The crazy part is that these two guys were very different from one another. If you asked either of the two how they achieved this success, they would tell you it's about culture and leadership. Same reason, yet two different styles.

- JK began his career out of high school as a courtesy-van driver before being promoted to service advisor. He moved forward as a body shop manager, then service director, and ultimately fixed operations director before moving on to another dealership. Without testing, it would be my opinion that JK's primary behavior is Social/Steady. JK is an extrovert, loves to talk, and loves to joke around. He enjoys being a servant to his team, often cooking breakfast or lunch for two hundred people. His outgoing personality attracts people. When asked how he recruits technicians, JK states that he calls his current technicians together, explains the reasoning for needing to add technicians, and then instructs his team to go find him someone. It works because of their high level of trust and respect for JK.

  JK's Organizational Structure would likely be Market/Clan. The primary philosophy is "Market Culture". JK has a focus on productivity and profits, having worked for years in a corporate dealership environment.

  He enjoys the philosophy but is not afraid to challenge it if it doesn't balance with the secondary culture that he nourishes. JK has created a secondary philosophy of "Clan Culture" that his team embraces. He and his team celebrate victories often and he encourages and empowers his staff to make good decisions. Work hard, celebrate!

- JR began his career as a technician apprentice. From a challenging childhood environment, JR was, and is, extremely focused on being the best at everything he did. JR is relatively quiet, yet a very good communicator and loyal to his people. He constantly challenges the norm but involves his team in doing so. His knowledge and patience for others attract people. All of the members of his team think of him as a friend (even ex-members whom he fired). JR's behavior style is most likely "Direct/Methodical." JR believes in mentoring and training technicians. He is very engaged with the technical schools and has created an amazing training process for developing new technicians.

JR's Organizational Structure would likely be Adhocracy/Clan. He has created an environment that empowers his team to constantly seek methods to improve every segment of the business. JR and his dealership are constantly focused on "state-of-the-art". Innovation is a top priority! He and his team are pioneers of testing different methods to better serve their customer guests and improve every component of the experience, from appointment process to reception, to repair, to cycle or duration time. It is also common to see technicians sitting with the dealer at lunch or company events. Not because they are required to, because they are very comfortable with doing so.

What is the common denominator in these two very successful Fixed Ops Directors?

Number One – CONFIDENCE! Their desire to embrace success for their staff with no fear or envy.

Number Two - Secondary Clan Culture! In each of these very different situations, these managers have created a focus on their objective while creating a "family" with their team members. The team members enjoy the ability to question management without fear of retribution.

In JK's situation (Market/Clan), the priority focus is on growth, profitability and having fun. But when a team member steps out of bounds, JK is very comfortable and confident with addressing the situation.

In JR's situation (Adhocracy/Clan), the priority focus is on team and innovation. He creates an extremely high level of confidence in his team members and constantly encourages entrepreneurship and innovation.

Perhaps, the best lesson that might be learned from this comparison is that Clan Culture may be valuable to create the environment of long-tenured, high-quality associates, but the primary Culture should be a focus on the business model. I have experienced many Clan Culture dealerships where the management has allowed the associates to create their own job description and/or business plan that could be called "the tail wagging the dog" or "inmates taking over the asylum". This is dangerous.

I call this a semi-true story because these are my observations and analysis from outside of these organizations.

In a recent study, 65% of employees said that they would forgo a raise to see their manager fired. Most of JK and JRs teams would take a bullet for them. The trust and respect for these individuals are amazing and mutual.

Of the 86 things on your daily/weekly/monthly list (a guess), what 10 items are most important? Are these items written down? Does every person on your team know what these items are? Are these the 10 items that should be most important? If you are focused on the correct items, there is an extremely good chance that these 10 items will solve most of the 76 other items.

With and for versus to and against! Include the appropriate members in decisions that affect them. The buy-in will be amazing. In this book, we will discuss building many processes. First and foremost, involve the affected staff members. For example, one of the biggest mistakes managers make when implementing production objectives is pre-assigning a number without agreement and commitment from technicians. When you do this, you may make changes to improve their ability to produce more hours (parts delivery, advisor training, etc.), only to create more phone and coffee breaks. We must secure buy-in from everyone involved.

The Starfish Story

An old man had a habit of early morning walks on the beach. One day, after a storm, he saw a human figure in the distance moving like a dancer.

As he came closer, he saw that it was a young woman, and she was not dancing but was reaching down to the sand, picking up a starfish and very gently throwing them into the ocean.

"Young lady"he asked: "Why are you throwing starfish into the ocean?"She responded "The sun is up and the tide is going out, if I do not throw them in, they will die!" He responded: "But young lady, do you not realize that there are miles and miles of beach and starfish all along it? You can't possibly make a difference."

The young woman listened politely, paused, bent down, and picked up another starfish and threw it into the sea, past the breaking waves, saying: "It made a difference to that one."

Though many of us are familiar with this tale, let it serve as a continual reminder that, as a leader, your influence on others is far more profound than you may comprehend. Recently, I was reminded of this when my friend published a book. After years of working together, he has evolved into an incredibly successful Fixed Ops Director, Chief Operating Officer, and a sought-after speaker at NADA. In an unexpected honor, he dedicated his book to me, acknowledging how I gave him a chance to prove himself when he was nearly homeless as a teenager. Looking back, it proved to be an astute decision on my part, though at the time, he was merely another starfish in the vast ocean. Who is the next starfish you're ready to save?

CHAPTER 2:
Managing the Chaos –
The Thermodynamics of Management

For many managers, the daily demands can be overwhelming. As a result, we are constantly reacting to situations. We will likely get really good at reacting to these situations, but the situations never change until we take the initiative to change them. Remember the definition of insanity:

"Doing things the same way, expecting different results."

Each time you implement a process or procedure, a technique should be implemented to assure compliance with the process or procedure.

A **Structured Operating Technique** and/or **Operational Operating Technique** should be considered for every process that you implement. Understanding these techniques will assist you not only in becoming a better manager of your time but also in making new processes work effectively. We will refer back to these techniques many times as we discuss specific change options in this book.

The **Structured Operating Technique** is the "Pendulum".

This is a process that is designed, created (written) and implemented, and when followed, should cause a predictable outcome with minimal management intervention. The Structured Operating Technique is the "Pendulum". Because the force, weight and motion are defined, the outcome is predictable for a given period of time. What is important to understand is "predictable for a given period of time." Unattended, even the best pendulum will eventually stop due to the friction created by air. The laws of thermodynamics confirm that there is no such thing as perpetual motion. Similarly, even the best Structured Technique will eventually deteriorate, if left unattended. But, for the most part, the results are predictable for a given period of time and require very little management intervention. Think of it as nudging the pendulum from time-to-time. A Structured Operating Technique example: Management gives each technician a flat fee per month for the purchase of their own shop supplies (for example, $100 per month). The technicians are now free to make their own buying decisions. (Note: The purchase of those supplies should be limited to supplies for which the dealership has current Material Safety Data Sheets [MSDS] on file).

In this example, the technicians can keep whatever portion they do not spend. Studies show that, on average, consumption drops almost 40% per technician, per month, as compared to a free-for-all unregulated shop supply distribution. Management has made a decision that has altered the outcome from the previous method of tracking shop supplies. This structured economic change requires very little management intervention.

An **Operational Operating Technique** requires hands-on management to maintain integrity and effectiveness. Because these Operational Operating Techniques require management interaction, these processes should be the most important processes that you have and should be used in conjunction with a Structured Operating Technique. If we hire a new employee and let them go to work without any formal direction, then we either have to constantly monitor and correct them or accept them to "create" their own job description. Then we wonder why they failed to meet our expectations.

As a manager, Operational Operating Technique is the "Juggler" act. It works great as long as there are not too many balls in the air at one time. A manager should focus on minimizing the amount of time spent in the Operating Technique. If possible, a manager should look to delegate some of the operational tasks to reduce the number of personal balls in the air. It is important that we learn to manage with a balance of Structured Operating and Operational Operating Techniques in our workplace. We begin by creating a process document or flowchart that will instruct our people to perform at the desired level. Then we decide when and how long we are going to spend managing this process in the operational mode. Now we are managing our time. Goodbye, juggler; goodbye, bull!

Combining Structured/ Operational Techniques

The most successful Service Managers understand that most processes require a combination of Structured and Operational Techniques. Without structured techniques, management will be involved in everything (100%) that happens. If we rely on every process to be structured, without any interaction from management, we are likely to be disappointed. The key is a balanced structured/operational process.

"Any system left to manage itself is in a constant state of decline"

Earlier, when we discussed the shop supply allowance concept, we should look at the challenges. While simple, we are likely to be confronted with theft problems (technicians claim that shop supplies go missing from their work area, and they probably do). In addition, some technicians will try to purchase supplies outside without an MSDS, and in addition, is the income taxable?

An example of a combined structured/operational technique would be a can-for-can shop supply policy. In this example, the technician turns in an empty can of brake cleaner, lubricant, etc., in order to get a new can. This does a **reasonable** job of assuring that the technicians are not taking shop supplies home. Management would need to conduct a review to ensure that the usage, by technician, is relevant to their production.

In the example of the can-for-can, a monthly audit should be done to: a) assure that the process is being adhered to; and b) compare the consumption for each technician who performs the comparable type of work.

Example: Bob and Jim are both transmission techs. They both produce about the same number of hours per pay period. Bob used 10 cans of cleaner last month, and Jim used 3. Why? Is Bob overusing cleaner, or is Jim building dirty transmissions? In this case, a Structured Technique managed the day-to-day activity, and an Operational Technique audited the outcome.

A manager can only juggle so many balls, so they focus on three or four items at a time. By utilizing a combination of Structured and Operational Techniques, the manager can designate the three or four items that are most important to the service department at any given time. Other management tasks can be delegated to others.

These techniques can prove to be very valuable to you as you move on your journey toward creating a solid, successful service department.

Step 1 of Managing the Chaos is to understand what is causing the concern or problem. Many times, the problem is caused by poor or a total lack of communication. How do we solve that?

Let's say that we have a concern with advisors getting adequate information for the technicians to perform diagnostics in a timely manner. Most manufacturers offer some form of diagnostic worksheets. If they do not, it is easy enough to create your own; your technicians will help.

Do your advisors possess a written job description or a detailed process document? If so, does that job description clearly outline the necessity of utilizing a diagnostic worksheet for designated concerns? Has this document been properly reviewed and signed by every advisor? In situations where an employee lacks a job description, we unintentionally place the burden of expectations solely on their own standards, rather than ours. A mere verbal policy is, in effect, nothing more than a suggestion, lacking the power of enforcement or clarity.

Step 2 is to determine and define how this process will be managed. Understand that all processes have to be managed. This is where the Structured Technique and Operational Technique are important.

In the example defined in Step 1, you created a Structured Technique by identifying the process, writing, and training each of the advisors in the process. In theory, this process should not require any follow-up, right? Wrong! Most of our advisors are humans and creatures of habit.

In Step 2, we design the process or rules for the Operational Technique. This is how we are going to manage the exceptions.

Maybe we ask our technicians or warranty administrator to log exceptions by advisor and concern type. You, or your designee, will review and counsel advisors on a daily, weekly, or monthly basis. This process must be in writing! When initiating this process, it may seem to consume more time and effort than apologizing to your customers for not fixing their cars, but this will eventually be a permanent solution, requiring minimal follow-up and fewer apologies. Key word "minimal" does not mean zero follow-up.

Anything Can Work! If you did nothing else as a result of reading this book but talk about improving productivity in every discussion, every day (sincerely), you are likely to see improvement in productivity.

There are very successful service departments that utilize dispatchers, electronic dispatch, teams, and/or groups. There are very successful service departments that use various work schedules. As well, there are very successful service departments that utilize various pay plans. Summed up, a well-defined, well-implemented, and well-monitored process will usually work. If we miss either one of these key items, the process may work for a while but will eventually deteriorate. In this book, we discuss many "ways" to develop and implement key processes. The number one cause of clearly defined and implemented processes failing is the lack of management intervention. Management must be extremely aware of the time required to fulfill this obligation. Every process that we implement will **require** a check and balance if we expect it to be successful.

Understanding the pros and cons of each technique will assist you in both managing your time and gaining positive results from your process.

As you begin to develop new processes, please remember that two of the biggest mistakes that a manager typically makes are:

1. Implementing a new process without putting it in writing. If it is a verbal implementation, you are leaving it up to each individual to interpret the process, which is dan-

gerous. An old mentor of mine had a favorite saying: "If it ain't in writing, it never happened." Once again, if it is not in writing, it is a suggestion.

2. Implementing a new process without considering what management actions will have to be implemented to assure that the new process is adhered to. Rarely does a new process work for any long period without having some level of management intervention.

The Flat Rate Pay Plan, as we know it, was designed as a Structured Operating Technique to cause the technician to be responsible for their own production. But, when left alone, with no operational support, we leave it up to the technician to determine their own objectives and abilities. The challenge is that this tends to create the perception that nobody really cares, which we will further discuss in Chapter Three "The Flat Rate Mentality". A successful Structured Technique always requires an Operational Technique. This is more traditionally known as "Inspect what you Expect"!

The laws of thermodynamics confirm that there is no such thing as perpetual motion. Even the perfect pendulum is subjected to a level of thermodynamics that creates drag, friction, and heat, ultimately stopping the pendulum if left unattended. I cannot think of a better analogy for management having a role in the maintenance of Structured Techniques.

As you create a process or technique to solve the challenge, you **must** create a technique to monitor performance. An example might be that you set technician or advisor production objectives. The technician and/or advisor agrees to accomplish their objective, and you have it in writing. You will typically see an immediate increase in performance. However, if left alone, the increase will be temporary. In this case, you would need a system to provide feedback daily. I cannot tell you the number of times that technicians have told me: "We've tried that before but it never works very long". This is a perfect example of expecting the Structured Technique to take complete control of managing the process. Remember, even the best Pendulum slows down (thermodynamics).

We must have an Operational Technique to support the process. The key is to maximize the "Pendulum" and minimize the amount of time as the "Juggler". With well-developed Structured and Operational Techniques, the manager can schedule time to manage the exceptions and minimize the amount of time spent. Example:

- Daily: review and counsel performance against production objectives (1 hour).

- Review and counsel Advisor performance, sales performance, and menu/mpi performance (0.5 hours).

- Monday: Audit Inspection Process (MPI)
  (0.5 hours)

- Are technicians following the process?

- Audit advisor Diagnostic Worksheet usage
  (0.5 hours)

- Tuesday: Review service performance month-to-date. Compare it to the pro forma and forecast (1 hour).

- Wednesday: Build a new process document
  (2 hours).

- Approach a new objective or correct a concern.

- Thursday: Implement the new process document.

- Train associates on the new document. Add to the playbook. (2-3 hours)

- Friday: Review work in process. Advisors should explain any repair orders that have been open for five days or longer (1-2 hours).

This sample illustrates a manager using less than 30% of their work-week creating and managing playbook processes. A schedule like this allows managers to transition from the position of "consumed-by-current-reality" to a position of true leadership.

When you discipline yourself to perform your duties in a fashion similar to this example, you begin to get your arms around your business, and you're able to climb off the bull. This Operational Review philosophy must be applied to every process that you implement; otherwise, you're wasting your time!

In Summary, as a manager, your task is to develop policies, processes, and procedures that your department operates by. The most successful managers develop policies, processes, and procedures as a structured operating technique whenever possible. The most successful managers then have time to create operational techniques to manage the policies, processes, and procedures. In the previous example, a properly onboarded flat-rate technician would have the following:

- Well-defined Job Description - Structured Technique (Technician understands expectations)

- Well-defined Pay Plan - Structured Technique (Technician understands how to make money)

- Agreed-upon Production Objective - Structured Technique (The technician understands the fairness of dispatch and the expectations of their production.)

- Daily production huddles – Operating Technique to review previous days/week-to-date performance

- Management Review and Counseling - Operating Technique (Checks and Balances of Structure)

> *"Whether you think you can, or think you can't – you're right!"*
>
> ***Henry Ford***

CHAPTER 3:
The Flat Rate Mentality

ONCE UPON ANOTHER TIME, a young man had completed a high-school auto shop program and spent his senior year in an on-the-job training program at a local dealership. He was top in class for his newly acquired knowledge and skills and, best of all, he was living his passion. After graduation, he continued working at the dealership, for a while, as an apprentice. Then he began working on flat rate, got married and started a family. Moving from hourly to flat rate was a great moment in this person's life. Finally, an opportunity to get ahead.

Life was mostly good, but as most young families experience, it was a paycheck-to-paycheck lifestyle. Most days, the flagged hours were good, but some days they were not so good due to a lack of work or getting stuck on a really difficult job. On these days, as this technician was driving home, his thoughts were "How am I possibly going to make this up?" or, "How am I going to pay my bills?" and, "Nobody seems to care!" If you were ever a flat-rate technician, you might believe this person was you! This is the beginning of what we'll refer to as the Flat Rate Mentality!

The Technician's Perspective

1. The Flat Rate Mentality begins with "Independent Contractor" belief. When we hire technicians, we offer them a wage that, we believe to be fair, competitive with the market and within our gross profit needs. While the technician may be appreciative of their new opportunity, their concept of the arrangement is probably different

than ours. The technicians' "reality" might be that you are renting them a "bay" or "stall". If you are paying them $30.00 per hour and your "door rate", "grid rate" or even, perhaps, "warranty rate" is $130.00 per hour, their perception is that they are paying you, the company, $100.00 per hour for the use of your stall or bay.

The lack of trust is further amplified by the belief that warranty labor times are purely budget-driven by the manufacturer, with no consideration of the actual repair time required. We know this isn't exactly the truth, but we're not really the important people in this perception.

First, we only wish that the $130 per hour was our effective rate, not to mention all of the expenses that are related to the production of that hour. While we know this is not the truth, it is the perception. Perception is reality in the mind of the perceiver! The perceivers are repairing cars in your shop.

2. The second Flat Rate Mentality factor is the "I'm alone to survive" belief. Many technicians feel alone in the world of work. Sure, they have buddies that they talk to, and even have beers with after hours, but they believe that no one else really cares whether or not they make a living. This belief is confirmed in their minds every time they are asked to do something for nothing. Whether it is scanning a vehicle for codes, shoveling snow, airing up tires, installing a license plate, or performing a multi-point inspection, they see it as us stealing their productive time. Now we know the technician probably wastes far more time in a day than they ever spend doing "freebies", but it is a perception. And perception is reality in the mind of the perceiver! Once again, the "perceiver" is repairing cars in your service department. The survival belief creates a lack of trust in other people and "the system".

While most technicians believe in the concept of inspections, overall, they lack trust that returning vehicles will be given back to them to perform the additional repairs. Further, a lack of trust in the entire flat rate system is created by the technician's lack of understanding of why customer-pay pays more time than warranty.

Understanding the Flat Rate Mentality

The Flat Rate Mentality is not really all about a pay plan. We have just allowed the pay plan to take all of the blame. It's about a culture and a very important focus that most successful companies and industries share. The focus is on productivity, but that's a secret. A secret because we don't manage it properly. Productivity has a major role in our competitiveness and, ultimately, our profitability.

This focus on productivity may come with some interesting new challenges:

Several years ago, I was hired as a consultant to visit a medium-sized dealership in a relatively small town in the Northeast. This dealership was suffering from very poor service absorption, and the service department was busy but barely profitable.

The technicians were all paid hourly and productivity was poor (averaged slightly less than 70%).

- The technician's morale was great: "I do whatever they ask me to, we all help each other."

- The atmosphere was definitely "family-like."

- The only person suffering was the dealer, the financial statement, and many times, the customer!

The dealer did not want to change his technicians to flat rate but was agreeable to an hourly compensation plan with a variable rate based on the previous month's individual productivity. We implemented production improvement processes and the new compensation plan to reward the technicians for their hard work. It was a success. Now that the productivity of the service department had increased, I returned and we introduced a multi-point inspection process to "feed-the-hungry-production-machine". When introduced to the new inspection process, the technicians argued: "Who's going to pay me to do these inspections?" I was shocked at first, but soon began to recognize this newly-identified behavior. These were "hourly" technicians with a whole new mentality…The Flat Rate Mentality!

Every "for-profit" business must have a focus on productivity. If you are an hourly-paid assembly-line worker, you are expected to assemble your portion of whatever you assemble in a designated amount of time. When the time is up, the line moves. If any of the assembly-line workers have not completed their task, the line is stopped. A supervisor will determine who failed, and counseling will take place. As we discussed in **Chapter 2**, the automated assembly line process is a Structured Operating Technique while the supervisor counseling is an Operational Operating Technique.

The Technician's Perspective on Customer Retention

Technicians believe in the logic and philosophy of customer retention. Unfortunately, the "Flat Rate Mentality" causes many a technician to believe that customer retention is someone else's responsibility. The "Subcontractor" belief says: I pay the dealership 100 bucks an hour to use their bay, the least they can do is keep me busy. The "I'm alone to survive" belief is: "That's someone else's problem, I have to get my "xx" hours, today."

Improving Customer Retention in a Flat Rate MentalityEnvironment

You might be lucky that you've survived! Face it…no-one has experienced the impact from competition more than the automobile business. More competition, both in nameplates and independent service providers has continued to gobble up our customer base and vehicles are much higher quality, causing less repair opportunities. Many of us sit back, business as usual, hoping for something good to happen. These attitudes allow Flat Rate Mentality to prosper. Improving Customer Retention in a Flat Rate Mentality environment involves CHANGE! We must learn to change.

Customer Retention must be the key focus!

Customer retention is critical to our future success. If you don't believe this, no one else will.

1. Set Your Vision - Your vision must be stronger than your current reality! When your vision is stronger than current reality, you will begin to find time to get off of the bull and begin implementation of new ideas. Many dealers and service managers have attempted, on many occasions, to implement change, only to hit a wall of opposition. The wall is "opposition to change itself", not necessarily what is being changed. If you understand why, you are doing something and believe from the bottom of your heart that it is the right thing – set it as your vision. Employees see this vision as strength and they will respect and honor the strength.

2. Communicate Your Vision - Develop a focus for your department! Through many years of studying dealership CSI, we've discovered that the primary difference between dealerships that are truly successful in customer satisfaction and those that are

not so successful in customer satisfaction is communication. The successful dealerships talk about CSI often, like every day, and it comes from the dealer down. Everyone understands the importance. In the fast pace of our everyday world, we tend to tell our staff what to do rather than set their vision. We must work "with and for" and not "to and against."

Saturday service to improve retention. As an example, many dealerships have had unsuccessful Saturday service for years. The dealer probably told the manager to open on Saturdays, and the service manager informed the staff. Week after week, Saturdays are sabotaged by advisors, technicians, and even managers who would like to see Saturdays stopped. Meanwhile, the independent service providers continue to enjoy Saturday as their busiest day of the week. What if you, as a manager, set your vision for Saturdays to be your biggest day, communicated this with all of your staff daily, and encouraged their feedback in making it happen. As you do this, remember that most people understand logic. And the logic in this case is that 60%+ of our customers defect, and the main reason is inconvenience. If you don't believe it, take a field trip to one of your Independent Service Provider competitors one Saturday morning.

3. Consistency in Communication - The #1 concern that employees express is a lack of involvement and communication. Employees will complain about having meetings, but they complain loudest about not having meetings. In fact, a lack of meetings reinforces a technicians sub-contractor and "all-alone" beliefs which is the opposite of what we want or need. Have meetings often, but remain brief. I recommend, and highly encourage, consistent daily technician meetings. These meetings allow discussion of the previous day's production, ongoing discussion of the "Vision" and encourages employees to be at work on time. Consistently means, if you are going to have daily meetings –

HAVE MEETINGS EVERY DAY. If you don't, you are showing a sign of weakness in your focus on the vision. Arrange meetings to not interfere with technician clock hours. If techs start at 8:00 am, have meeting at 7:50.

How to Create "Customer Retention Focused" Flat Rate Technicians

Implement Production Objectives – Every flat-rate technician shows up to work, each day, with a number in their head. That is the number of flat rate hours that they need to produce to be able to make a living at their expected level. At the end of the day, we can tell if they accomplished this number by the look on their face, happy or frustrated. The frustrating days support the "I'm alone in this world to survive" theory. No one else really cares. What are the alternatives? Implement formal Production Objectives. There are three ways to do this, two wrong and one right:

1. Base objective on Technician Skill: A-Skill = 10.0 hours; B-Skill = 9.0 hours; etc. "WRONG!" It may penalize great technicians who are not extremely productive.

2. Calculate and tell the technician what they need to produce. WRONG! No buy-in from technicians.

3. With and for! Negotiate and agree on plan. RIGHT! Production Objectives, when properly implemented and managed, help tremendously in conquering the "I'm alone in the world to survive" mentality. But feedback is mandatory. As we discussed earlier, performance against production objectives must be monitored and communicated daily, weekly and monthly. Morning Production Meetings, we discussed earlier, are the perfect opportunity to do so. Without feedback, the objective is only a number.

Daily meetings give management an opportunity to discuss a plan of action to resolve poor productivity prior to it being too late. It makes dispatch inadequacies obvious. This gives the technicians the assurance that someone else cares. In addition, production objectives provide the service department the information needed to effectively schedule and load work into the shop. Now the advisor can better forecast accurate promise and/or status times. The financial bonus that a typical service department, who correctly implements production objectives, realizes an eight to twelve percent increase in productivity. Do the math on that one! Most technicians, dealers or managers won't complain about an 8-12% raise. In addition, morning meetings give the managers an opportunity to assure that technicians arrive on time and the chance to share any additional communication. More information on implementing Production Objectives in **Chapter 6**.

Summary

While fair and focused pay plans are very important, we sometimes expect pay plans to do everything. This will not happen. Remember Newton's theory of physics: "For every action, there's an equal reaction." As it comes to technicians, we can manage their action by paying them hourly and "whipping" them into producing. Or, we can compensate them based on production (flat rate) and manage the reaction by helping them to be a part of a bigger picture and showing care and concern for their needs.

If we consider three important factors in EVERY decision that we make, we will succeed in this endeavor:

1. Will it support and improve customer loyalty and retention?

2. Will it support and improve employee loyalty and retention?

3. Does it support the dealership's **profit needs**?

While we mentioned a couple of specific ways to improve in this quest, there are many, many ways to build on this. These examples might include specific recognition or rewards for improvements in customer retention; funding or supplementing 401(k) programs with profit sharing. Most of all, we must include retention in every meeting and conversation that we have with our staff.

CHAPTER 4:
The Fundamentals of Service Department Profitability and Building a Proforma

The old saying of "If you're not moving forward, you're backing up" has never been truer than today! Costs and competition are constantly increasing. It seems that your business is either growing or shrinking. There is no middle. So how do you improve your bottom line? You could wish for better results. Or you can understand what causes profitability in a Service Department, then plan and implement changes for improvement. According to Paul Simon's song, there might be "50 ways to leave your lover", but there are only 10 ways to improve Service Department profitability. Labor Sales and Net Profit are not an element, but a result. To improve these results, we must look upstream at the elements that control change.

These ten ways to improve service department profitability have been divided into two parts, or "Fundamentals," for a reason.

In the Service Department, we sell labor hours! "Nothing happens until a technician picks up a wrench!"

Fundamental #1 is Production Capacity. Labor rates and gross profits mean nothing until labor hours are produced. Fundamental #1 is about all of the components that cause billable labor hours. This fundamental includes 5 Production Elements, that cause labor hours to happen. These 5 elements are the stepping stones that produce, sellable, flat-rate-hours.

Capacity Element #1: Tech Hours Worked Per Day

Capacity Element #2: Days Worked in a Month

Capacity Element #3: Calendar Utilization %

Capacity Element #4: Technician Productivity %

Capacity Element #5: Number of Technicians

Fundamental #2 is Production Conversion. In Fundamental #1, we calculate and determine the number of production hours (inventory) that are likely to be sold from the daily labor time-bank inventory. While production hours are the lifeblood of the service department, we cannot spend production hours. Fundamental #2 includes the five Conversion Elements that determine, or cause, these production hours to become sales dollars, gross profit dollars, and ultimately net profit dollars. The Conversion Elements are:

Conversion Element #1 - Effective Labor Rate $

Conversion Element #2 - Gross Profit %

Conversion Element #3 – Labor Adjustments $

Conversion Element #4 - Expenses %

Conversion Element #5 – Other Gross Profit $

In Chapters 5-8, we will discuss these 10 elements, how to calculate or determine these numbers, and ideas for improvement. We will also discuss building a Proforma to better understand your current situation. Then, in Chapter 9, we discuss "ways" to improve your dealership's performance in some or all of the elements of the 2 fundamentals by reverse-engineering your pro forma.

PROFIT FUNDAMENTALS & THE 5X5 ELEMENTS

Many Service Managers were promoted from advisor positions. Many others were promoted from technician positions. It is likely that a former advisor might be more familiar or comfortable with Production Conversion, as advisors are typically focused on gross profit and effective rate. A former technician will be more familiar with Production Capacity, as technicians are typically focused on flat-rate hours and all of the things that cause or prevent them. Great managers will be good at both. This book is designed to provide that assistance.

Building a Base Proforma

If you were to go to the bank and request money to open or purchase a business, the banker is most likely going to ask you for a pro forma, regardless of what type of business. A pro forma is simply a breakdown in financial terms of what causes the business to make revenue and how your purchase or changes are going to impact the business. Ultimately, in this case, it will help the bank understand its risk in loaning you the money.

All businesses should have a pro forma. In the case of a service department, a pro forma helps you understand what causes your current performance and helps you identify actions or processes that could lead to improvement. Without a pro forma, a business will look like a "wish or hope" business. This is where one might make changes but "wish" or "hope" they will get good results. Banks don't make wish or hope loans, and you shouldn't risk your career on it.

In our recommended pro forma, the two fundamentals are divided so that in Fundamental #1, Production Capacity is broken down into the five production elements. To improve shop hour output, one or more of these five capacity elements must change. Then we move to Fundamental #2, Production Conversion, which is broken down into five conversion elements. These are the numbers that you use to convert and manage hours to dollars.

How do the Business Development Center (BDC), advertising, and marketing affect the pro forma? Fundamental 1, Production Capacity, is the tool to manage the inventory of hours available in the service department. Your BDC, your advertising and marketing strategy, and multi-point inspections are all tools to improve supply. The ideal situation matches scheduled hours to the capacity created with the assistance of the pro forma.

Next is a copy of a Service Proforma. It is broken into three categories: 1) Production Capacity Leading Elements; 2) Production Conversion Leading Elements; and 3) Results. The right-side column, "New Situation," is an area to propose changes to the Leading Elements and predict the results of the proposed changes.

Proforma

	SERVICE SALES / PROFITS		CURRENT		NEW SITUATION	
			BASE		CHANGES	RESULTS
	Leading Indicators			#		
FUNDAMENTALS — **PRODUCTION CAPACITY**	Clock Hrs. Worked Daily			1.1		
	Days Worked Monthly	X		1.2		
	Calendar Utilization %	X		1.3		
	Productivity %	X		1.4		
	Technician Hour Value	=				
	Number of Technicians	X		1.5		
	Total Hours	=				
CONVERSION	Effective Labor Rate $	X		2.1		
	MONTHLY LABOR SALES $	=				
	Gross Profit %	X		2.2		
	LABOR GROSS PROFIT $	=				
	Labor Adjustments	-		2.3		
	Monthly Expenses $	-		2.4		
	LABOR NET PROFIT	=				
	Other Gross Profit	+		2.5		
RESULT	MONTHLY NET $	=				
	ANNUALIZED	X				
	Total Annualized Service Net Profit $	=				
	ANNUAL IMPROVEMENT $	=				

> *"If the only tool you have is a hammer, you tend to see every problem as a nail."*
>
> **Abraham Maslow**

CHAPTER 5:
Fundamental #1 – Production Capacity

1.1 - Production Element #1 - Technician Hours Worked per Day

This is the number of hours, on average, that a technician is scheduled to work each day, according to policy. For example, if all of your technicians work 8-5, Monday through Friday (we'll discuss Saturdays in "Days Worked in a Month") and are allowed to take one hour for lunch, then you have 8-hour work days.

Hours Worked per Day

Start Work Time		End Work Time		Total Hours		Lunch / Breaks Hours		Daily Hours
8:00	:	5:00	=	9.0	-	1.0	=	8.0

Variations: Let's use an example where we have 12 technicians. Six technicians are scheduled to work 8 hours per day, and six are scheduled to work 10 hours per day. The math would work as follows:

Modified Work Schedule

# Techs		Scheduled Hours		Total Hours	
6	X	8.0	=	48.0	(a)
6	X	10.0	=	60.0	(b)

(a)		(b)		Total Hours
48.0	+	60.0	=	108.0

Total Hours		Total Techs		Worked per Day
108.0	÷	12	=	9.0

In this "hours-worked-per-day" calculation, you will want to use scheduled hours and not actual clock hours. Deviation from scheduled or expected clock hours will be identified in the productivity measurement.

NOTE: In this calculation, disregard Saturday and Sunday hours unless they are full days, fully staffed as a regular workday. We will calculate weekends in the "Days Worked per Month" calculation.

Where do I find this information? This is totally based on your company policy. It should be written. Many dealerships offer options for technicians, such as 8-hour workdays, 4-10 hour workdays, or even 3–13-hour workdays.

1.2 – Production Element #2: Days Worked in a Month

This is the number of days, on average, that the service department is open and the technician would be scheduled, by policy, to work. For example, if the dealership is typically open Monday through Friday (we'll discuss weekends later), the calculation will be as follows:

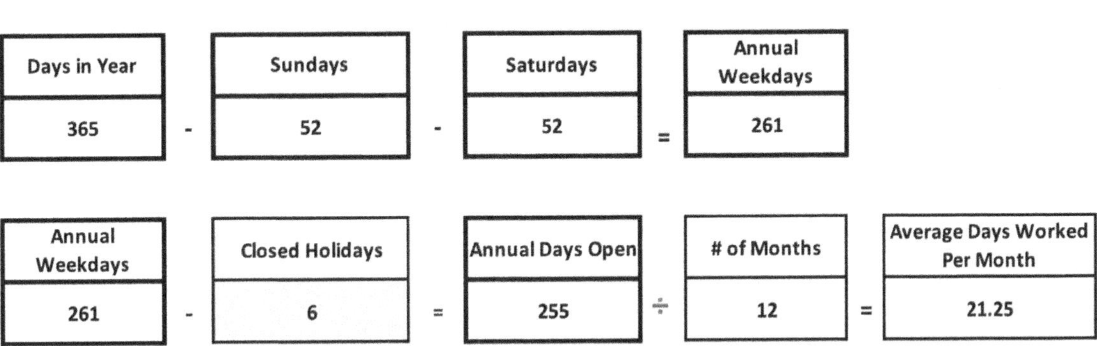

On our sample Proforma, we will record this as 21.25 worked days per month. Now let's look at a couple of variations (examples):

EXAMPLE 1 - Saturdays

In this example, 50% of the technicians work each Saturday and do not get a day off during the week. The techs work from 8:00 a.m. until 12:00 noon on Saturdays (half a day).

In this calculator, we start with the 52 annual Saturdays, multiply by the percentage of workday (4 hours = 50%), and multiply by the percentage of technician staff on hand (50%). The result is an annual equivalence of 13.0 days per year. This equates to an average of 1.08 additional workdays per month.

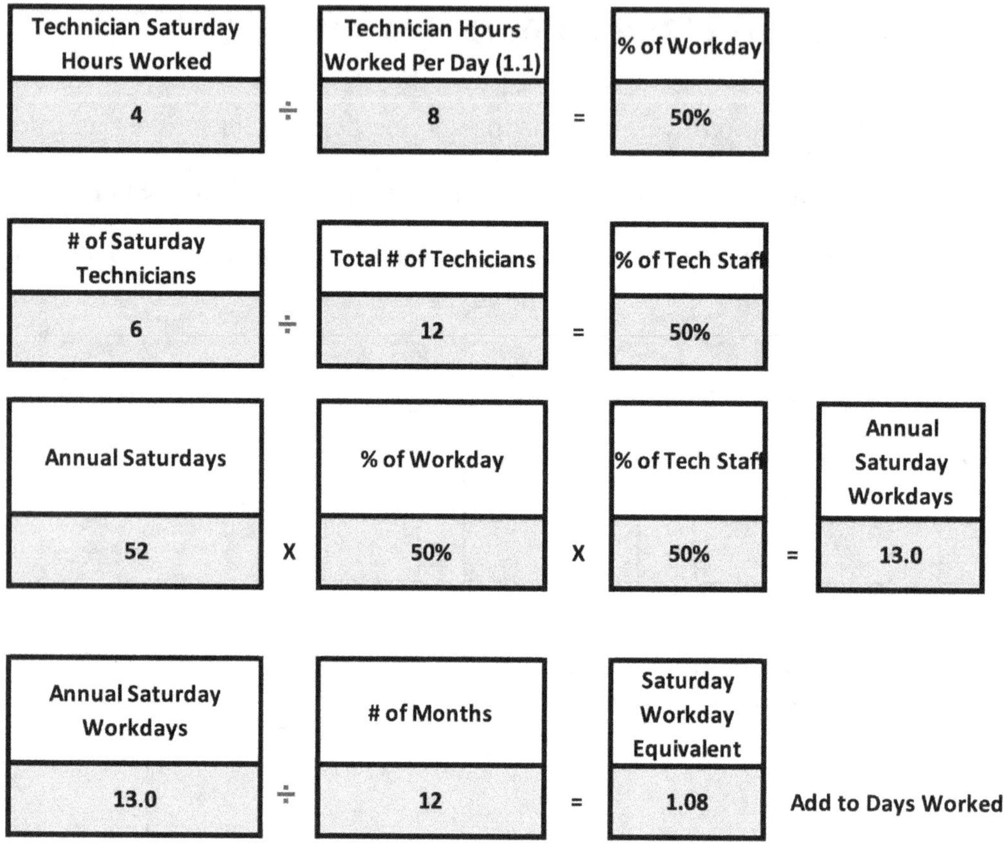

EXAMPLE 2 - (Modified Workdays)

This is an example of a modified workday shop with 12 technicians. This method could be used for multiple reasons:

1. Attract technicians with a flexible, four-day workweek.

2. Improve opening times to accommodate more customers.

3. Add additional technicians in limited space shops; for every four technicians in rotation, there is the possibility of adding an additional technician.

Example:

6 Techs work 5–8-hour workdays

6 techs work 4–10-hour workdays

Days Worked per Month / Modified Work Schedules

5-8 Hour Workdays	Days in Year		Weekend Days		Annual Weekdays Off		Annual Workdays
	365	-	104	-	0	=	261.0
	Annual Workdays		Closed Holidays		Annual Days Open		# of Months
	261.0	-	6	=	255	÷	12

Average Days Worked Per Month = 21.3

4-10 Hour Workdays	Days in Year		Weekend Days		Annual Weekdays Off		Annual Workdays
	365	-	104	-	52	=	209
	Annual Workdays		Closed Holidays		Annual Days Open		# of Months
	209	-	6	=	203	÷	12

Average Days Worked Per Month = 16.9

TOTALS	# Technicians		Days Worked per Month		Total		
	6	X	21.3	=	127.5		
	6	X	16.9	=	101.5		
					229.00	÷	12

Average Days Worked Per Month
TOTAL = 19.1

1.3 – Production Element #3: Calendar Utilization

Calendar Utilization is the percentage of the month or year that the technician(s) would ordinarily be available to work and are actually working. The difference is the number of days, or percentage of days, that the technician is absent due to:

- Vacation

- Training

- Sickness / Personal Time

- Attrition (if used)

Vacation– When calculating an annual average-month pro forma, count the number of technicians who are eligible for 5 days, 10 days, and 15 days (if applicable) of vacation. Also, count the number of technicians who are not yet eligible for vacation. The pro forma sample dealership has 12 technicians who have 95 combined vacation days.

Training– This is the estimated number of days that your technicians will spend in training during the year. In the pro forma sample dealership, it is estimated that a total of 80 days will be spent in training.

Sickness/Personal Time– This will be based on your dealership's policy. In this example, the policy is five days per employee. Expect each employee to take these days unless you have an incentive in place to reduce usage. This will be discussed in the next chapter.

Attrition– You may or may not choose to project and/or measure attrition in Calendar Utilization, but it is a good method of understanding the cycle time of losing a technician. For example: If we lose a technician on the tenth working day of the month and do not replace him/her in the same month, it would reduce the calendar utilization by .5% (22.33 monthly work-days – 10 days-worked = 12.33 days of attrition).

12.33 ÷ (22.33 X 12 techs = 267.96) = .46%, rounded to .5%

A good rule of thumb to consider would be:

If you lose a technician with the full intention of replacing him or her, count it as attrition days.
This will help you better manage attrition cycle time.

If you lose a technician for the purpose of downsizing, do not count him or her as attrition. Rather, change the technician count on your pro forma.

Technician Missed Days Calculator

Annual Days of Vacation

0 days	5 days	10 days	15 days		Total Techs
2	4	3	3		12
0	20	30	45		95 Total Days

Total Vacation Days		Estimated Total Annual Training Days		Estimated Annual Technician Attrition Days		Annual Personal Days (per Tech)		
95		80		75		5.0		
(7.9	+	6.7	+	6.3	+	5.0	)=	25.8
Average Annual Vacation Days		Average Annual Training Days		Average Attrition Days		Personal Days		Average Missed Days (per Tech)

In this sample dealership, the manager is estimating that in a year, he or she will have an attrition vacancy in his or her current technician staff for 75 days. While this is a bit of a SWAG (scientific wild-ass guess), it establishes a goal for replacing technicians and/ or a better job of retaining technicians.

Calendar Utilization Calculation

Average Days Worked per Month		# Months		Total Days Available (per Tech)
22.3	X	12	=	268.0

Total Days Available		Average Missed Days (per Tech)		Average Actual Work Days per Tech		Total Days Available		Calendar Utilization
268.0	-	25.8	=	242.1	÷	268.0	=	90.4%

In the sample dealership, 9.6% of the time, a technician will be absent (100%-90.4%). This is very common. Using the calendar utilization calculation can assist you in scheduling. In this sample dealership, for every 10 technicians that you employ, on average, one will be absent every day. Could you possibly schedule these "time off" events to accommodate an additional tech?

Where do you find the information?

1. Count your technicians.

2. Based on the tenure of your technicians, calculate the total number of annual vacation days. Your payroll person could probably assist you.

3. Based on the company policy, calculate the number of sick and/or personal days likely to be taken. Once again, your payroll person could probably assist you.

4. Calculate the average number of days that each technician will be away from the dealership for training.

5. If you choose to predict attrition, review your recent history to determine how long it takes to replace a technician.

Calendar Utilization can be a good reason to break down your annual forecast pro forma into a monthly forecast. In the previous example, we determined that the dealership had a total of 309.6 annual missed technician days (25.8 x 12 technicians). How could you plan to allocate those days across the 12 months to reduce the impact on your labor sales in any particular month? Schedule training for slower months. Incentivize certain times of the year. Vacations for slower months or allocate only a certain number of vacation days allowed for each month, first come, first serve?

1.4 – Production Element #4: Technician Productivity

PRODUCTIVITY: Productivity is the efficiency of the production of goods or services expressed by some measure. Every successful business has some level of focus on productivity. While the workers in a production line may be paid an hourly wage, their productivity is controlled by the speed of the line.

Productivity is the single **MOST** important measurement in a service department! In a Service Department, we sell labor hours. The measurement of Productivity is mandatory. Some manufacturers or other circles call it Productivity, others call it Proficiency. Regardless of the terms, the calculation is the same. In summary, Productivity is about the number of hours that a technician produces in a stated period (day, week, etc.), divided by hours available. In this book we will refer to it as Productivity. The calculation is:

HOURS PRODUCED divided by HOURS WORKED = PRODUCTIVITY %

The technician produces 35 hours in a week. The technician works 40 hours:

(35 ÷ 40 = 87.5% productivity)

Productivity Calculator

Hours Flagged		Hours Worked		Productivity %
35.0	÷	40.0	=	87.5%

Productivity percentage is the number of billed hours divided by the number of hours worked. What is important for us to understand are the two components of Productivity:

Component 1 – Technician Utilization

Component 2 – Technician Efficiency

Productivity by Technician

Technician Name	Hours Flagged		Hours Worked		Productivity %
Billy	45.0	÷	40.0	=	112.5%
Fred	42.6	÷	40.0	=	106.5%
Ralph	41.7	÷	40.0	=	104.3%
Lucy	36.5	÷	40.0	=	91.3%
Jimmy	37.6	÷	40.0	=	94.0%
Suzy	35.6	÷	40.0	=	89.0%
Freddie	26.7	÷	40.0	=	66.8%
Bubba	23.6	÷	40.0	=	59.0%
Lubi	25.6	÷	40.0	=	64.0%
TOTALS	314.9	÷	360.0	=	87.5%

In **Chapter 6**, we will discuss in detail, the techniques for a better understanding and opportunities for improvement in the two components of productivity.

Once again, the terminology may be different depending on the product brand, but the calculation is the same.

Where do I find this information?Using your DMS reports for Technician Hours Flagged (divided by) Technician Daily Work Hours (times) hours worked in a defined period. In the case of this example, it is 5 days, or 40 hours. This will determine your overall productivity.

1.5 – Production Element #5: Number of Technicians

Technicians are the lifeblood of the service department. Technicians create productivity. Productivity causes labor sales. Labor sales cause parts sales, etc. Everyone needs technicians, right? How many? How do you determine that?

First, we need to understand how many technicians we might need. Once we understand this, we can focus on hiring, recruiting, and training technicians. In Chapter 6, we will discuss "ways" to determine how many technicians you might need, the skill levels required, and other factors involved in planning headcount.

As we create our Proforma, it is important to understand what constitutes a "Technician". A technician is a person that creates "billable hours". This could include: Mechanical Technicians, Quick-Lube or Quick-Service Technicians, Detail and/or Internal Technicians (if hours are billed through the Service Department).

Using the Proforma

By recording our dealerships current situation on our Proforma, we can use all of the Leading Elements of the Profit Fundamental #1 – Production Capacity to determine the best way(s) to improve our production. Based on the sample calculations we did for each of the Production Capacity Leading Elements, this is what the current, or base, situation would look like. In this example, if our information is correct, this dealership will produce approximately 1695.7 production hours in an average month.

	SERVICE SALES / PROFITS		CURRENT	
			BASE	
	Leading Elements			#
PRODUCTION CAPACITY	**Clock Hrs. Worked Daily**		*8.0*	1.1
	Days Worked Monthly	X	*22.33*	1.2
	Calendar Utilization %	X	*90.4%*	1.3
	Productivity %	X	*87.5%*	1.4
	Technician Hour Value	=	*141.3*	
	Number of Technicians	X	*12.0*	1.5
	Total Hours	=	*1695.7*	

You can verify the accuracy of your pro forma Total Hours calculation by running an hours-flagged report on your DMS for a 12-month period, divided by 12. While it is okay to use a shorter period for this calculation, a longer period (6 months to a year) is likely to be more accurate.

It is highly unlikely that your pro forma will have an exact match to your financial statement, as different DMSs round in different ways. If your pro forma calculation does not closely agree with your DMS, one or more of your Leading Elements are incorrect:

1. Clock Hours Worked - Are all technicians scheduled to work an 8-hour workday?

2. Days Worked Monthly - Do all technicians work the same schedule? Are Saturdays calculated properly?

3. Calendar Utilization - In your comparative month(s) from your DMS, was the Calendar Utilization abnormally high or low? If you are only using data from one or two months, you may be using data from a month that had a lot of vacations, training and/or sickness. Typically, the best annual calculation for Calendar Utilization is average vacation days, sick days and training days. Did we lose technicians during the month?

4. Productivity - When calculating your Productivity, make sure that you include every person who flags and bills flat rate hours. This would include lube technicians, detailers and apprentices, if they flag production hours. If you have a service department that does a significant amount of quick lube and/or detail, I recommend that you create the overall proforma to assure that your numbers are correct. Then create a Proforma for the 2 or 3 different departments (mechanical, quick lane, detail).

5. Technician Count - Are we counting the number of people that bill hours? Once again, this would include lube technicians, detailers, and apprentices, if they bill flagged hours.

Once you have completed this Base Situation Proforma, you should have determined why your production capacity is what it is. In Chapter 6, we will discuss ways of improving each of the key elements of production capacity.

CHAPTER 6:
Improving Production Capacity

What is the best way or ways to increase your production capacity? Lets begin by understanding your **supply** versus **demand** situation. When we improve our production capacity, it may act like a big vacuum cleaner. The work gets done. Let's look at the following questions:

1. How many non-hold, non-working carryovers do you average each day?

2. How far out are you scheduling appointments?

3. Are your advisors able to sell additional work (ASRs)?

These could be predictors of demand that exceeds supply. As a rule of thumb, you can add the number of appointments that are beyond three days, and the number of non-holds, non-working carryovers, and multiply by your average hours per RO; you can establish a baseline for additional production needed. When your demand exceeds the supply, the quality of the work mix degrades. This is not necessarily the quality of the repairs but the quality of the work coming in. If it is difficult to get their vehicle serviced, the customer is going to go elsewhere unless it's a warranty repair or a very difficult diagnosis. Advisors tend to avoid selling additional work due to the fear of making the backlog problem worse.

If the demand currently does not exceed the supply, but you need to increase labor sales, then you would want to consider processes that improve customer convenience as well as production capacity. These might include extended hours and/or better scheduling.

When making plans to improve production capacity, highly successful service directors typically involve their staff in creating the best solutions for their situation. This establishes the buy-in needed to make the changes successful.

1.1 - Leading Element #1: Improving Technician Hours Worked per Day

It has been my experience to see service technicians work an 8-5 shift with 1 hour for lunch and maybe a 15-minute break in the middle of the morning. This would really be a 7:45 workday. In addition, many times the meal truck drives in at the beginning of the break. Twenty technicians line up to get breakfast. By the time the technicians consume their breakfast, 30 to 45 minutes are wasted. Now we have a 7:15 to 7:30 hour workday. What options are there to improve on this?

Non-compliance to the hours-worked-per-day policy will lower productivity. If a technician is scheduled to work 8-hours-per-day, then he or she arrives to work 30 minutes late, spends an extra 15 minutes at lunch, their utilization is already reduced by nearly 10%, before anything else happens. The math:

45 minutes per day x 21.3 workdays =

16 hours per month x $110 effective rate =

$1760 per month, lost revenue per technician.

Ideas to improve hours worked:

Add a half-hour to the workday and have the technicians break at two different times, maybe 9:00 and 9:20. This would reduce the line at the meal truck. If you add a half-hour to the start of the day, make sure there is work available to begin the day.

Reduce lunch from 1 hour to a half an hour. This could be a means of increasing 6.3% in an 8-hour-per-day shop by working 8.5 hours per day. Or, this could offset break. Do you have the work to make this a sensible change?

Do technicians have work upon arrival in the morning? Many times, technicians will say that there is no work when they get there on time, so they come in late. Could you stage new and/or used vehicles in their bays? Should we take appointments earlier? Maybe we have a technician who has family responsibilities that prevent them from being at work at 8:00. Should we schedule this person to an 8:30-5:30 shift? Flexibility can build tenure.

Modified Work Schedules - 4-10-hour-day rotation. This would change your work-day to 10 or 10.5 hours (1/2-hour lunch), but will reduce the days-worked-per-month. If you are looking to extend your hours to attract more customers, this could be a good alternative. Technicians would rotate days off during the week.

1.2 - Leading Element #2: Improving Days Worked in a Month

Weekends- Increase Saturday hours and/or the number of Saturday technicians. While this, generally, is not a very popular topic, could you grow your Saturday (or Sunday) business? One of the biggest challenges with weekend hours is scheduling. When left to advisors, Saturday service scheduling is usually sabotaged. Top-performing service departments use BDC or open up online scheduling for weekend hours.

The following graphs illustrate the impact that extending the Saturday workday by 2 hours would have on increasing the monthly days worked by .55 days. This equates to 41.7 additional hours per month. Is this a worthwhile effort? Do you need additional customers? Would this additional exposure improve your availability for these customers?

Current Situation

	SERVICE SALES / PROFITS		CURRENT	
			BASE	
	Leading Elements			#
PRODUCTION CAPACITY	Clock Hrs. Worked Daily		8.0	1.1
	Days Worked Monthly	X	22.33	1.2
	Calendar Utilization %	X	90.4%	1.3
	Productivity %	X	87.5%	1.4
	Technician Hour Value	=	141.3	
	Number of Technicians	X	12.0	1.5
	Total Hours	=	1695.7	

Add 2 hours to Saturday

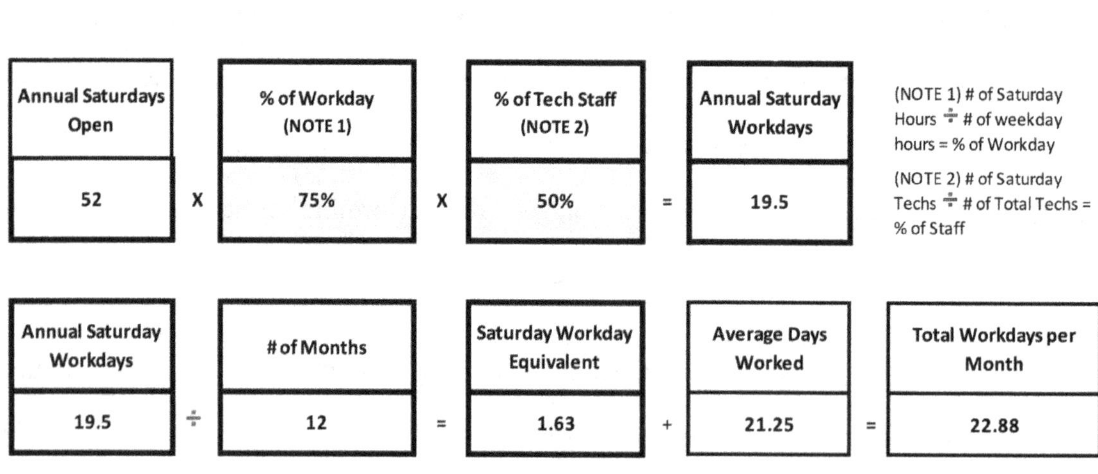

New Situation

	SERVICE SALES / PROFITS		CURRENT		NEW SITUATION	
			BASE		CHANGES	RESULTS
	Leading Elements			#		
PRODUCTION CAPACITY	Clock Hrs. Worked Daily		8.0	1.1		8.0
	Days Worked Monthly	X	22.33	1.2	0.55	22.88
	Calendar Utilization %	X	90.4%	1.3		90.4%
	Productivity %	X	87.5%	1.4		87.5%
	Technician Hour Value	=	141.3			144.8
	Number of Technicians	X	12.0	1.5		12.0
	Total Hours	=	1695.7			1737.4

Holidays –Does it benefit your situation to open on certain holidays (likely Memorial Day and Labor Day)? If you are currently closed for both of these days and decide to open, the Days Worked benefit would be .17 days per month. Probably not worthy of the negative employee response that would accompany this decision.

1.3 - Leading Element #3: Improving Calendar Utilization

Calendar Utilization can be very volatile when calculated monthly. We calculate the annualized Calendar Utilization but it can vary wildly during the course of the year. It is the role of service management to manage this. We can do this in two ways:

1. Build Monthly Proformas – In January, we may have no vacations; in June, we may have five vacation weeks. Calendar Utilization is going to vary drastically.

2. Budget Missed Days – Determine the likelihood of training throughout the year, by month. Then, allocate vacation days by month and distribute them by seniority or first-come, first-served. Peak seasons should be considered, of course.

Without this, you are likely to have huge deviations in calendar utilization.

Ideas to Improve Calendar Utilization

It is a relatively common practice to buy vacation from technicians. It improves Calendar Utilization and technicians seem to like it. If forced to take vacation time off, some technicians will spend the week working on cars in their garage. Buying all or part of their vacation will improve your calendar utilization by reducing the number of vacation days.

Align Vacation with Training - In Florida, many of the technician training centers are located at or near Orlando. What would be the response if a technician could go to training and take vacation at the same time? Go to training, take the family, get paid double; the family goes to Disney. Wow! Improved calendar utilization. What is your opportunity? Whether a family interest or personal interest, can we wrap the two together?

Many dealerships will buy back unused sick and personal days at the end of the year. Improved calendar utilization!

Some dealerships deliver a vacation check to the technician on their anniversary date. The technician might go out and buy the new hunting rifle that he or she has been dreaming about, leaving no money left over for vacation. This can be very effective in improving Calendar Utilization but be cautious of the long-term burnout implications that might exist.

Reduce technician attrition by using the methods and examples described in Chapter One – Culture. Make your technicians a proud partner in a great team. Create a file of potential candidates. It is a statistical fact that the highest number of job-seekers is January and February. Always go through the interview process, even though you may not be seeking someone at the time. If you have a solid candidate, sell them on your service department. Take them on a tour, introduce to positive influencers. Then, explain that you do not currently have any openings, but you would like to stay in contact.

1.4 - Leading Element #4: Improving Technician Productivity

Productivity percentage is the number of billed hours divided by the number of hours worked. Some manufacturers call this measurement "Proficiency". Regardless of what we call it, the measurement is the same. This area is typically the greatest area for improvement once you understand the components.

Productivity consists of two extremely important components: Technician Efficiency and Technician Utilization. Once again, many manufacturers refer to these components as "efficiency" and "productivity." We'll refer to this as the European model. The measurement and calculations are the same; only the names have changed.

Because it is so difficult to measure these two components individually, they are usually just calculated as one. Nevertheless, it is important that we understand each of these components:

Calculation for Productivity: Hours Flagged ÷ Hours Worked = Productivity %

Efficiency % X Utilization % = Productivity %

European Model: Efficiency % x Productivity % = Proficiency %

Technician Efficiency– The ability of a technician to actually perform the repair in the time allocated by the appropriate labor time guide. Technician Efficiency is primarily affected by proper dispatch and training. Has the technician received adequate training to perform the repair? Does the dispatch system distribute the job to the most qualified technician?

Calculation for Efficiency: Hours Produced
or Flagged ÷ Actual Job Hours Worked =
Technician Efficiency

Manufacturers generally require dealerships to perform accurate clocking for warranty repairs. If this same process could be followed for customer-pay and internal repairs, it is likely that you could get close to determining your dealership's actual technician efficiency.

Measuring efficiency can be a challenge. A true measurement would require that a technician clock off to take a coffee or smoke break. And, after all, we are not here to beat our technicians into being more productive. Rather, let's help them make more money. When asked, technicians generally have an idea of the hours in a day that they are not actually working on vehicles.

Technician Utilization– This is very different from Calendar Utilization. Technician Utilization is the percentage of time that the technician is present and actually working on vehicles. Utilization cannot be over 100% and likely will not even reach 100%. At 100%, we would be indicating that the technician is working on vehicles every moment that they are present, which would be awesome but borderline impossible. Utilization is primarily affected by scheduling, technician punctuality, advisor communication, and parts availability. Why are technicians at work and not working on vehicles? There are many reasons, but they could include: no work at start time, waiting in the parts department, advisors not getting enough information, tool trucks, meal trucks, locating special tools, etc. In most dealership service departments, this is a huge opportunity.

Calculation for Technician Utilization: Hours Actually Working on Vehicles ÷ Hours on Clock or Scheduled = Technician Utilization

Once you have assimilated this information, use the following calculation:

Hours Scheduled to Work – Wasted Hours = Hours Utilized

Hours Utilized ÷ Hours Scheduled to Work = % Utilization

This graph estimates Technician Efficiency and Utilization based on the estimated wasted hours. This is an example of a technician that is estimated to average 1.5 hours-per-day "idle". The word idle means: not being utilized. While 1.5 hours per day may sound excessive, think about the discussion in section 1.1 (earlier in this chapter). In that example, the technician arrives 30 minutes late (no work), takes an extra 15 minutes for lunch or breaks. This is common! And this example represents 45 minutes per day 3:45 hours per week, before we have any discussion about parts delays, advisor delays, etc.

Productivity Calculator

Hours Flagged		Hours Worked		Productivity %
35.0	÷	40.0	=	87.5%

Calculator to Estimate Technician Efficiency

Hours Worked		Wasted Hours		Hours Utilized
40.0	-	7.5	=	32.5

Hours Utilized		Hours Worked		Technician Utilization %
32.5	÷	40.0	=	81.3%

Productivity %		Technician Utilization %		Technician Efficiency %
87.5%	÷	81.3%	=	107.7%

NOTE: Benchmarks suggest that journeymen technicians should be between 125% and 150% efficient, and master technicians between 150% and 200% efficient, depending on the warranty/customer pay work mix. This would suggest that a master technician that flags 40 hours per week is only being utilized 50%-75% of the time. What an opportunity!

Improving Technician Efficiency

Training Focus

- Online training - Is the technician fulfilling their obligation for online training? Are they getting paid?

- Classroom training – Are we scheduling promptly?

- Mentorship – Do we have strategies to cross-pollinate skills?

Dispatch System

1. Are jobs going to the most qualified technicians? Do not allow a "gunslinger" approach. Gunslinger is when the dispatcher just wants to eliminate their pressure by saying "It's in the shop."This can cause big-time quality problems.

2. Is the "dispatch" system incentivized by individual production? Whether you are using a dispatcher or not, you have a dispatch process. Does this process pay attention to production, including technician efficiency and quality?

Improving Technician Utilization

This is likely the biggest opportunity to improve production capacity in your dealership. It focuses on wasted time, and most of it is completely within your control. While we listen to concerns about manufacturers' labor times, how much time do our technicians spend actually repairing cars and trucks? Most dealerships are able to increase their production capacity by well over 10% when they understand and implement these ideas.

Improving Technician Utilization is about reducing the waste. In the service department we sell labor hours. Lost Technician Utilization is about the amount of time that our technicians are unproductive. This can be huge!

What causes lost utilization? Examples:

- Technicians arriving late or leaving early due to poor scheduling (no work). Can we pre-stage vehicles to begin their day? (Carryovers, PDIs, etc.)

- Parts waiting and/or availability issues - Could we print pick tickets and pre-pull and/or deliver parts? Do we have overnight parts checked in and available when technicians arrive?

- Dispatching quality – See **Dispatching Options** in this chapter.

- Advisor obtaining and recording inadequate information – Could we use technicians to help us develop and implement training materials, including diagnostic worksheets?

- Moving vehicles in and out of the shop – How long does it take a technician to retrieve a vehicle? If it takes more than three or four minutes, could we number the parking spots or have a porter bring the vehicles in?

- Tool trucks and food trucks – Schedule food trucks and tool trucks for the lunch hour, prior to the start of the workday, or at the end of the workday.

- Special tool availability – Put special tools under lock and key or move them to the parts department to be checked out. Your parts manager may not like this idea, but he or she should be reminded that higher technician productivity equals more parts sales.

- Technical information delays – Are there alternatives to technicians holding on the phone for technical assistance? (Apprentice, warranty administrator, etc.)

- Customer approval tools. Can we speed up the process by electronically texting estimates to our customers? There are many tools available, and feedback is overall positive.

Ideas to Improve Productivity

Production Objectives– There are various ways to implement Production Objectives. Most common is the pay period "hit" levels…example $1.00 retro at 45 hours, $2.00 retro at 50 hours, etc. The problem is that certain technicians will always hit and others will hit every other pay period by manipulating the flagging of repair orders. Also, in many dealerships, the very best technician(s) may not be a 50-hour technician. Is it okay to pay him/her less?

Here is the recommended technique for setting production objectives. When implemented properly, this process creates the buy-in needed to assure success. In addition, this process, when managed properly, typically creates a 10-12% improvement in Productivity.

With and for.

Prior to the individual discussions, it is important to discuss with the group or each member to explain the "why" of what you are about to do. The "why" might include any or all of the following:

- Underproductive technicians are not making enough money due to obstacles.

- A backlog of work is making it very difficult to sell additional jobs.

- "It's hard to hire good technicians."

- "Unable to schedule work properly due to no management of supply (hours)."

- Unable to manage dispatch or distribution due to daily management.

Step 1: Determine each technician's previous personal production performance.

- Calculate the average personal production hours for 12, 24, 26, or 52 weeks, per technician: (Hours Flagged ÷ Total Days Worked) = Average Production Hours per Day.

- Average Production Hours per Day ÷ Daily Work Hours = Productivity %

Hours Worked per Day	8.0			

Technician Name	Days Worked	Hours Flagged	Average Flagged Hours per Day	Productivity %
Billy	60	558.4	9.3	116%
Fred	58	607.8	10.5	131%
Ralph	60	550.1	9.2	115%
Lucy	56	496.9	8.9	111%
Jimmy	59	488.7	8.3	104%
Suzy	60	440.5	7.3	92%
Freddie	55	396.5	7.2	90%
Bubba	60	388.6	6.5	81%
Lubi	57	320.5	5.6	70%

Step 2. Meet with each technician individually to discuss their production. The meeting should be similar to this:

- "Good morning, Jimmy, I wanted to take a few minutes to talk about your productivity. I did a calculation for the last 12 weeks and your productivity is 104% or about 8.3 hours per day on average. Does that sound right?"

- "Are you happy with this? Or, could you do more?" 95%+ the answer will be more.

- "What could be done to help you produce more?" Expect to hear responses based on efficiency or Utilization (too much time at the parts counter, poor write-up, parking lot issues, etc.). Write down and review each item.

- The response to each item should be either:

  - "I will fix that." Maybe it is implementing and managing Diagnostic Worksheets to get better information. Maybe it is staging cars, pre-pulling parts, or delivering parts to the technicians.

  - "I will look into that and get back to you by (date)." Maybe this is the feasibility of adding a parts runner. You could compare this technician's concern to other technicians to decide if it really should be addressed.

  - "Welcome to the car business." An example might be backordered parts. "I hate that too, but unfortunately, there is little that you and I can do about that."

- It is extremely important that we take the technician's concerns, seriously!

- "If I can change or fix the things that we discussed, could you produce more?" Again,95% of technicians will respond with a "Yes". "How much more do you think you could do?" most of the time, the answer is going to be 2+ hours per day. Your focus should be set on the following targets:

  - Technician is currently in top 1/3 producers - 5% improvement

  - Technician is currently in middle 1/3 producers- 10% improvement

  - Technician is currently in lower 1/3 producers – 15% improvement

PRODUCTION OBJECTIVE CALCULATOR

Hours Worked per Day | 8.0

Technician Name	Days Worked	Hours Flagged	Average Flagged Hours per Day	Productivity %	Increase %	Objective
Billy	60	558.4	9.3	116%	5%	9.7
Fred	58	607.8	10.5	131%	5%	10.9
Ralph	60	550.1	9.2	115%	5%	9.6
Lucy	56	496.9	8.9	111%	10%	9.7
Jimmy	59	488.7	8.3	104%	10%	9.1
Suzy	60	440.5	7.3	92%	10%	8.1
Freddie	55	396.5	7.2	90%	15%	8.4
Bubba	60	388.6	6.5	81%	15%	7.7
Lubi	57	320.5	5.6	70%	15%	6.8
	525	4248.0	72.8			80.0

- So, I'm going to make the changes that we discussed, and I will research and respond to you on the other item(s). We are also going to implement "Production Objectives." This will help me monitor and assure that the changes are working. I certainly believe that you can produce those 2 hours that you suggested, but let's take baby steps. I would like to set your objective for 9.1 hours. That's a 10% improvement. Are you good with that?

Step 3. Create a Production Report similar to the template below or use the DMS Productivity Report. Designate someone to populate this report daily, either early in the morning or at the end of the day. This report should be used each morning to meet with each technician, either individually or in a huddle. The purpose of this meeting is to understand each technician's productivity and determine if any assistance is needed. If a technician has had struggles, you may want to designate some "gravy" to help that technician get back on track. This process is called "Feeding by Design". Feeding by Design must be clearly understood by all technicians in order to prevent jealousy or hard feelings. This process is also an opportunity to congratulate the technicians who are performing well.

<table>
<tr><td align="right">Day of Week -</td><td>1</td><td colspan="8">1-Mon, 2-Tue, 3-Wed, 4-Thu, 5-Fri, 6-Sat, 7-Sun</td></tr>
<tr><td align="right">Hours Worked per Day -</td><td>8</td><td colspan="8"></td></tr>
</table>

Technician's Name Week 1	Daily FRH Obj.	Days Present 1-7	Weekly Sub Total Total FRH	Weekly Sub Total Total CLK	Total Obj.	Objective Obj. %	Objective Hrs +/-
Bill Smith	12.0	4	46.7	32.0	48.0	97%	-1.3
Lucy Smith	10.0	4	40.7	32.0	40.0	102%	0.7
John Jones	9.5	4	36.8	32.0	38.0	97%	-1.2
Sally Jones	10.5	4	44.8	32.0	42.0	107%	2.8
James Jones	7.5	3	21.6	24.0	22.5	96%	-0.9
John Smith	8.0	4	28.6	32.0	32.0	89%	-3.4
				0.0			
				0.0			
				0.0			
				0.0			
				0.0			
				0.0			
				0.0			
				0.0			
				0.0			
				0.0			
DAILY TOTALS	57.5		219.2	184.0	222.5	98.52%	-3.3
			119%				

Dispatching Options

Proper dispatching is critical to the success of a service department. The person(s) or equipment that are in charge of this function must be focused on three primary elements:

1. Skill match: An understanding of the skills needed to perform the repair and the skill set of each technician.

2. Customer promise time – Understanding the customer's expectation for completion time and calculating a start time that will best accommodate this.

3. Technician production needs (Production Objective)

There are, basically, six ways that are used to dispatch.

1. Jobs on desk or free-for-all

2. Electronic Dispatch, manned or unmanned

3. Central Dispatcher

4. Shop Foreman Dispatcher

5. Advisor Dispatch

6. Group or Team Leader

Free-for-all dispatch is where the work orders are laid out on a desk or in a rack. The technicians come to the desk and pick their next job. This is the honor system. This technique should be avoided. Even when jobs are positioned in different "stacks" for each technician, this method invites and encourages technician manipulation and "cherry picking" jobs which will result in production inconsistencies, missed promise times and employee turnover. I have arrived at service departments before opening and witnessed the top producing technicians selecting their jobs-for-the-day prior to anyone else arriving. This method also encourages advisors to hand-walk jobs to certain technicians.

PROS: No dispatch expense.

CONS: Little control over promise times.

Imbalance of Productivity – Manipulation by technicians.

ELEMENTS:

1. Skill Match – Poor for most, except the favored.

2. Promise Times – Poor

3. Production Needs – Poor for most, except the favored.

While **electronic dispatch systems** have come a long way, they should NEVER be left unattended! These systems can do a pretty good job of matching skills and promise times. In addition, these systems can do a good job of providing job status access for customer inquiries. I've yet to see a system that can completely fulfill technician production needs. Electronic dispatch will assign a tech the next job, regardless of the production needs. Unfortunately, all jobs are not created equal. Maybe, with AI, that will come. In addition, it is not an uncommon situation to see technicians all go home and leave an unassigned waiting customers in the customer lounge. If no one requests a job, the computer is not going to go grab someone and hand them the job. I've witnessed technicians that would look at jobs in the queue and then sit at their toolboxes until the jobs ahead of their desired job are pulled. Lost utilization, labor inventory lost forever!

PROS: - Manages Skills

Good job status availability.

CONS: - Does not understand personal needs (feeding by design).

No pressure to get jobs done.

Technicians learn how to manipulate. (Many technicians are gamers.)

ELEMENTS:

Skill Match – Good

Promise Time – Poor

Production Needs - Poor

Central dispatchers can work well when managed effectively. The primary benefits are good status communication, as there is a central point of command. Another benefit is the ability to offset poor-performing service advisors without doing excessive harm to the technicians. The negative is that, left unchecked, dispatchers may have a tendency to take care of their friends. To combat this, it is best practice to base a large portion of the dispatchers' pay on each technician achieving their production objective. Under pressure, dispatchers may turn into "gunslingers," handing out jobs to anyone who will take them in order to get them off of his or her desk. While a pay plan that is weighted to individuals hitting their objectives is a Structured Management Technique, it is important that service management have an Operating Management Technique to verify compliance. Also, what is the plan to fill this position with a qualified individual during the dispatcher's absence?

PROS: - Central point of contact for status.

CONS: Potential favoritism if not controlled.

Gunslinging jobs to underqualified technicians - initial personnel expense and need for backup.

ELEMENTS:

Skill Match – Poor unless managed by a pay plan.

Promise Time - Fair

Production Needs – Good if managed by a pay plan.

Shop Foreman/Dispatcher- The Shop Foreman certainly should have a great understanding of the technician skills. The question is whether or not this person has the time to pay attention. Much like using a dispatcher, we must have pay plans and controls in place to eliminate favoritism.

PROS: - Understanding of technician skills

CONS: Favoritism of technicians unless structure and pay plans prevent this from happening.

-Difficulty in customers getting job status

Advisor Dispatch– The Basic Shop or Simple Support configuration uses the advisor(s) to dispatch to the individual technicians in their work group. This requires a very skilled advisor, as it is important to understand the skills of each technician.

PROS: Savings on dispatcher or group leader expenses.

-Advisor has complete control of their destiny.

CONS: Requires a highly skilled advisor to balance dispatch with customer write-up responsibilities.

Group or Team Leader– Lateral Support or Team System type Advanced Production Systems typically use a Group Leader(s) or Team Leader(s) to dispatch the work assignments. The theory is "who would know the abilities of each tech more than someone who works alongside of them?" This method of dispatch generally does get the jobs in the right hands and/or recognizes the need for assistance in the event the skill is lacking. In larger shops, the drawback is communication. Unlike a dispatcher that is the central point of contact, a shop with multiple groups or teams will have multiple lines of communication. This requires a very proactive process of communication between the advisor and customer. Failure to do so will result in customers being caught in a loop if requesting vehicle status.

PROS: Great understanding of technician skills, efficiencies, and promised times.

CONS: - Difficulty for customers requesting status.

Potential dispatch unfairness if objectives are not managed.

"Backup plan" required for an absent advisor or group leader.

Vehicle Inspection Process

When we increase our production, we can create a hungry hour-machine. So, we must have a solid Vehicle Inspection Process, including returning the vehicle to the original technician for repairs. We often wish that our technicians were more consistent in the inspection process, but we need to realize that most technicians have never had any formal training on the inspection process. So, let's stop wishing and fix it. Here is a best practice for creating and implementing a formal Vehicle Inspection Process:

Designate, solicit volunteers, or elect a group of technicians to be a Process Implementation Team (PIT Crew). Generally, the Inspection PIT should consist of a manager, an advisor, and 1-3 technicians (depending on the size of the shop), including a lube technician, the best technician in the shop, and the most outspoken technician. With the PIT Crew's guidance, go through every single item on the inspection document and write a description of how that inspection should be performed. Also, identify whose role it will be to perform that particular inspection (example: in some dealerships, the technician tests batteries; in others, the advisor tests the battery; and in others, a porter tests the batteries). You might be surprised by the different opinions on how tire tread depth should be measured. This helps eliminate the controversy.

Determine what constitutes a "Red" or "Yellow" in a non-tire or brake condition situation. Generally, teams decide that "Red" means it needs to be done now or before the next scheduled service visit. The customer may have additional issues or breakdowns if ignored. "Yellow" is usually defined as preparing for this at the next service visit or two. This allows the customer to prepare for the expense, while many will choose to have the repair done now.

Determine what constitutes a "Red" or "Yellow" as it relates to oil leaks. Typically, PIT teams conclude that a seepage is "Yellow", whereas, a leak that drips would be Red.

Determine what constitutes a "Red" or "Yellow" relating to flushes and fluid exchanges. Many managers believe that these services should be primarily sold at write-up, based on time or mileage, using the menu. Therefore, a fluid exchange should only be marked "Red" if there is a failure of the component related to the fluid. Advisors often blame technicians for rubber-stamping inspections rather than actually looking for issues. This usually results in poor sales efforts by the advisor. Having a policy for fluid exchanges usually will improve this issue.

The manager's role is to keep logic and reason in the process and constantly remind the PIT Crew that every decision made should consider the fairness to the customer, the technician and the dealership. If it's fair to all, it is probably the right decision.

Once the process is written and agreed upon, arrange a meeting for all technicians. The manager introduces the new process, explains its importance to our business and customer retention, and then asks the PIT Crew to go over the document.

Solicit input from each member of the staff and set a date for implementation. Measure the results! Just like with the implementation of Production Objectives, it is critical to measure and manage your process. If it's not worth the manager's time, then it's not worth the staff's time!

Create a written policy for returning vehicles to the technician who made the recommendation whenever possible. Technicians regularly lack confidence that this will happen. Creating a written policy assures that everyone understands the procedure and helps create comfort in the technician's mind.

1.5 - Leading Element #5: Improving the Number of Technicians

The first question that we need to ask ourselves is, Why and how many? As a rule of thumb, if you can increase the overall productivity by 10%, for every 8 technicians that you currently employ, you gain the equivalent of 1 additional technician. If you currently employ 16 technicians and improve productivity by 10%, it's the same as adding 2 technicians. Would it be worthwhile to hire a parts runner or train and demand that advisors use Diagnostic Worksheets and stage vehicles to accomplish this? In addition, "everything is funny, with a pocket full of money"! Well paid technicians are more likely to talk it up with their peers. This can create a source for recruiting technicians.

The second question is about stall utilization. The common belief, at one time, was 2 bays per technician, so if my shop has 20 bays, then I needed 10 technicians. We would call this 2-1 or 50% stall utilization. In the last couple of decades, many alternatives have found to be successful. Lateral Support Groups can easily improve stall utilization to 3-2, which is 1.5 stalls per technician or 67% stall utilization. Teams can improve stall utilization to 1-1, which is 1 stall per technician or 100% stall utilization, because multiple technicians can work on the same vehicle. The standard that we see in most well-performing shops is 3-2 or 67% for non-engine/transmission technicians and 2-1 or 50% for technicians that perform primarily heavy repairs. Extended work days (4-10s, 3-13s, etc.) and double shifts can improve stall utilization even further. While very difficult to manage, there are dealerships that have 1-2 or 200% stall utilization. The stall utilization question is: "How many technicians do you have versus how many technicians do you need?" Once you can determine this, you can determine the best path forward.

There is also a term defined as Stall Productivity Utilization. This calculation is based on the hours produced per stall or bay. NADA benchmark is 75%. This means that every bay should produce 6+ hours per day. If two technicians share three stalls, the objective would be to produce a minimum of 18 hours per day. Remember, this is a benchmark. A benchmark is a number. If your stall utilization is different, understand why?

Now, assuming that you still need technicians, what skill level do you need? Here is a skill level guide to help determine this:

Step 1 - Technician Skill Summary

Step 1 – List Technicians and evaluate their diagnostic/repair skill level in the 10 key areas, 0-2 (0=unskilled; 1=semi-skilled, can perform basic diagnosis and repairs; 2=fully skilled, competent in diagnostics and repairs)

Step 2 – Add the score for each technician in total skill points.

Step 3 – Add TOTAL SKILL POINTS, divide by 10 (9 if you do not have diesel), then divide by the number of technicians. Your answer should be between 0 and 2.

TECHNICIAN SKILL SUMMARY

Ratings:
2.0 - Fully Qualified.
1.0 - Partially Qualified.
0.0 - Non Qualified

TECHNICIAN NAME	Electrical	Infotainment	Drivability	Climate Control	Brake Repair	Steering and Suspension	Engine Repair	Manual Transmission	Automatic Transmission	Diesel Engine	TOTAL SKILL POINTS
Billy	2	2	2	2	1	1	1	0	0	0	11
Fred	2	2	1	2	2	2	1	1	1	0	14
Ralph	1	1	1	1	2	2	2	2	2	1	15
Lucy	1	2	1	1	2	1	0	0	0	0	8
Jimmy	1	1	0	0	1	0	2	2	2	2	11
Sugy	1	2	1	1	2	1	1	0	0	0	9
Freddie	1	1	1	1	1	1	1	0	0	0	7
Bubba	1	1	0	0	1	0	1	0	0	0	4
Lubi	0	0	0	0	1	1	0	0	0	0	2
TOTALS BY COLUMN	8	12	7	8	13	9	9	5	5	3	79

Skill % Level	Electrical	Infotainment	Drivability	Climate Control	Brake Repair	Steering and Suspension	Engine Repair	Manual Transmission	Automatic Transmission	Diesel Engine
	44%	67%	39%	44%	72%	50%	50%	28%	28%	17%

Fully Qualified Score	# of Skills	# of Techs	Skill Level %
2.0	10	9	44%

In this example, the skill level is .88 or 44% completely skilled (79 ÷ 10 ÷ 9 = .88).

The first impression would be that either this dealership's work mix is very high maintenance (56%+) or they are underskilled, which takes us to the next calculations.

Arguments to the Skill Summary

Technicians who are trained and skilled should be willing to use their skills! Many times, dealerships reward technicians for their training achievements. The concern with this highly respected achievement is that it is not unusual for technicians to achieve these training objectives only to attain maximum compensation and not to actually perform the repairs for which they are trained. Maybe we should request or require technicians to perform the skills in which they are certified, at least to some level! While we understand that their optimum efficiency may not lie in these areas, maybe we could provide skill incentives?

Step 2: Technician Skill Demand

A – Run a DMS Op-Code or Repair Order Detail report for the most recent 30 days, or just grab a representative stack of 1-2 weeks of customer pay and warranty repair orders to first determine the percentage of the repair work mix (including warranty repair orders):

Determine the percentage of operations that are purely maintenance or competitive (oil change, rotate, balance, batteries, fluid exchanges).

Subtract the maintenance work mix percentage from 100%. In this example, 120 ROs yield 200 labor lines (note: multiple warranty lines to complete a single repair equal one labor line).

In this example, 88 labor lines are basic maintenance = 44.0% (100% - 44.0% = 56.0% repair labor lines).

B – Multiply 2.0 (Maximum Skill Points) by the percentage of repair operations and compare it to the calculation in step 1. In this example, 2.0 x 56% repair mix would determine that, in theory, we need a minimum overall skill level of 1.12 in order to smoothly accommodate the business requirements that we have. This is a good reference, but it does not take into account the size of the repairs (in hours).

REPAIR ORDER OP-CODE LINE COUNTS

TOTAL LINES	Electrical	Infotainment	Drivability	Climate Control	Brake Repair	Steering and Suspension	Engine Repair	Manual Transmission / Clutch	Automatic Transmission	Diesel Engine	Maintenance and Basic Recalls
200	22	12	10	8	19	12	14	2	11	2	88

WORK MIX % of LINES

Total Skilled Lines	Electrical	Infotainment	Drivability	Climate Control	Brake Repair	Steering and Suspension	Engine Repair	Manual Transmission / Clutch	Automatic Transmission	Diesel Engine	Maintenance and Basic Recalls
112	11%	6%	5%	4%	10%	6%	7%	1%	6%	1%	44%

Please note the work mix of 6% for automatic transmission. This next calculation will assist you in planning the number of skilled technicians that you need in order to process vehicles in a timely manner and optimize the productivity of your staff. You could also break this down into individual skills:

Calculate the percentage of repair operations for a particular type of repair. (Example: "Automatic Transmission" = 6% of total work lines; in a shop of 9 technicians, the shop would need .67 or 1 transmission technician to fulfill skill lines.) Before we rely on the calculation, let's consider that different skill repairs (transmission, engine) require longer average times to perform. Because of this, we will calculate the weighted skill demand.

Production Weighted Skill Demand

In the next step, we calculate the actual average hours for each repair line type to determine the percentage of the hours produced by automatic transmission repairs.

Based on 100% productivity, the 456.9 total hours would indicate that these 200 lines are based on a sample of about 6.35 days of work (456.9 ÷ 9 technicians ÷ 8.0 clock hours = 6.35 days). At 100% productivity, we will need 1.82 transmission technicians (92.4 transmission hours ÷ 6.35 days ÷ 8.0 tech hours per day). Alternatively, you can calculate as follows: 9 total technicians X .20 (20% of total hours) = 1.8 technicians that are transmission skilled. That is a pretty substantial difference when compared to only 6% of lines. In our sample dealership, we have 2.5 technicians who are transmission-skilled, which should fit the need. However, we must acknowledge that these technicians also perform other types of repairs. This can be especially important when you look at maintenance and basic recalls. In this dealership, 44% of the labor lines fit into the maintenance/recall category but only create 15% of the production, which, according to the calculation that we did for transmissions:

68.0 (maintenance hours) ÷ 6.35 (days) = 10.71 hours per day.

You will want to make sure that you're not overstaffing for this number of hours. It is fairly common for service departments to overstaff lube technicians, which affects productivity (supply exceeds demand). If we have issues with many oil changes coming in at the same time, we need to either improve our scheduling or pass some of these to the main repair techs. Remember: A $15.00 per clock hour technician at 50% productivity has a true cost of $30.00 per hour.

A lesson we can learn from the airlines

As we discussed in Chapter 4, nothing financially happens until a technician begins to produce billable time. Our inventory is time. Unlike parts inventory, if that time is not sold today, it does not carryover to tomorrow. It vanishes and is no longer available. Many times, in many dealerships, we tend to book capacity based on someone else's capacity (service advisors in most cases). In a Production Driven Culture, we should understand our capacity and do our very best to meet that.

Interesting enough, our business is very much like the airlines. What is the inventory of an airline? Seats! The challenge is, that when that aircraft's doors close with empty seats, they are unsold inventory lost forever…obsolescence. So, what do the airlines do to avoid this obsolescence? Overbook! If you have spent much time in airports, you have probably heard the call from the airline willing to pay $2,3,4 or $500 for anyone willing to take a later flight because this flight is oversold. Why would it make sense to oversell and pay someone $500 for a $400 ticket?

Overbooking is all about historical data and algorithms. Mathematically, this flight averages --% of the passengers not to show. This could be from a combination of missed connections and last-minute travel changes and the airline is measuring this. As a result of this measurement the airline overbooks. The theory being "for every seat that we buy back from travelers, we have eliminated 9 seats flying empty" or whatever their math is.

Many of our service departments under-book with the belief that we will always have walk-in's and emergencies. While true, you will also have no-shows. The questions that we should ask ourselves is "What is the average % (of hours) that are walk-ins and emergencies?" And, "What are the average number of no-show hours?" If we understand this, we can do a more accurate job of booking and avoiding technicians running out of work. When you measure the data and book accordingly, we will overbook from time-to-time and may need to deploy a couple loaner cars, but the offsetting benefit will be additional labor hours. Other times, we can use walk-ins as "standby" to fill in for the shortage of production hour supply. With most DMS's and/or scheduling systems, it is relatively easy to measure no-shows and walk-ins once you have a good understanding and focus on your production supply (objectives).

CHAPTER 7:
Profit Fundamental #2 – Conversion

Profit Fundamental #2 – Conversion is about how we convert the Production Capacity, or billable hours, into Labor dollars and ultimately Net Profit dollars. Once the Production Capacity has been determined, there are 5 Leading Conversion Elements that affect the amount of labor dollars and net profit dollars. We cannot spend flat rate hours. Nor do flat rate hours have significant value until the transaction goes through conversion. Once the production has happened (hours produced), Conversion is the elements that cause the production hour transaction to turn into labor dollars, gross profit and ultimately, net profit. Once labor hours are created, the ability to change or improve labor dollars, gross profit and/or net profit, would require change of one or more of these Conversion Elements. These elements are:

Conversion Element #1 - Effective Labor Rate $

Conversion Element #2 - Gross Profit %

Conversion Element #3 – Labor Adjustments $

Conversion Element #4 - Expenses %

Conversion Element #5 – Other Gross Profit $

2.1 - Conversion Element #1 - Effective Labor Rate

Effective Labor Rate is the calculation of Total Labor Sales divided by the Number of Hours Billed. If our service department charges the customer $250 for labor and the technician flagged or billed 2.0 hours, then our calculation is ($250 ÷ 2.0) or $125 per labor hour billed.

Effective Labor Rate consists of three components:

- Customer Pay Effective Rate

- Warranty Effective Rate

- Internal Effective Rate

The total of these three effective rates is known as the Overall Effective Rate or Combined Effective Rate. The breakdown of these rates is as follows:

- Customer Pay – the labor amount charged to customers, on average, per flagged hour. Most non-hi-line dealerships use two or three different rates for Customer Pay labor:

- Repair, Grid, or Door rate – this is the highest labor rate charged to customers. These are typically repairs that require a high level of skill and training.

- Maintenance rate – this is the rate, or average rate, charged for maintenance items such as oil changes, filter replacements, etc. This is typically the lowest rate.

- Competitive rate – this is the rate, or average rate, charged for competitive items such as brake jobs, alignments, batteries, and fluid replacements based on comparisons with the competition. The labor rate for this type of service is typically higher than maintenance but less than the "Door" rate.

Depending on the maintenance/repair work mix, it is not unusual to see overall customer pay effective rates that are 75% +/- of the "Door" rate.

1. Warranty – the labor amount paid by the manufacturer for warranty repairs. Depending on the option chosen by the dealership and/or the laws of the state, the dealership typically has a choice of a rate that automatically increases annually based on the GDP (Gross Domestic Product), CPI (Consumer Price Index), or is calculated on the dealership's current "Door" rate.

2. Internal – the labor amount billed to the new and used vehicle departments for pre-delivery and reconditioning services. Best practices from many dealerships suggest that the internal rate should be exactly the same as customer pay. Using this method may produce a reduced overall effective rate for internal versus customer pay. This is due to the fact that reconditioning usually involves higher-than-average competitive operations.

The easiest way to calculate your current effective rate is to run a report in your DMS. It will typically be called "Labor Sales Report" or "Effective Labor Rate Report."

2.2 - Conversion Element #2: Gross Profit %

Gross Profit is the dollar amount after the cost-of-sale is subtracted from the effective labor rate. In the case of labor, cost-of-sale is the amount paid to the technician(s). The calculations are as follows:

Total Labor Sales $ – Technician Cost $ = Gross Profit $

Gross Profit $ ÷ Total Labor Sales $ = Gross Profit %

There are two components to this element: Effective Labor Rate and Technician Cost. While Gross Profit % (GP%) can be found on the financial statement or DMS reports, it is important to recognize that the overall cost-of-sale and GP% are going to be weighted by productivity. Here is an example:

Technician Name	Hourly Rate	Hours Flagged	% of Total Hours Flagged		Contribution
Billy	$ 28.00	46.0	13%	=	$3.69
Fred	$ 30.00	41.5	12%	=	$3.57
Ralph	$ 30.00	44.0	13%	=	$3.79
Lucy	$ 24.00	38.5	11%	=	$2.65
Jimmy	$ 30.00	39.8	11%	=	$3.43
Suzy	$ 22.00	37.2	11%	=	$2.35
Freddie	$ 22.00	35.5	10%	=	$2.24
Bubba	$ 20.00	37.6	11%	=	$2.16
Lubi	$ 16.00	28.5	8%	=	$1.31
	Total Hours	348.6	Weighted Cost of Sale		$ 25.18

In this example, the Average Hourly Rate is $24.67 (Total Hourly Rate ÷ # of Techs), but your actual cost is higher ($25.18) due to the higher production of the higher paid techs.

2.3 - Conversion Element #3 – Labor Adjustments

At some period of the month (usually at payroll time), the office will make adjustments to reconcile the technician payroll.

These adjustments are created by unapplied time and/or adjustments to gross profit. This is usually a result of either:

- Paying hours to technician but not billed to the customer or expense account, or

- Amounts paid to hourly or salary technicians but not billed to the customer or expense account.

EXAMPLE: Lube Tech makes $15.00 per hour, 40 hours per week. ($15.00 x 40 = $600)

Lube Tech produces 32.0 hours for the week and is costed at $15.00 per hour.

($15.00 x 32 = $480)

$600 - $480 = $120 would be the unapplied time or labor adjustment.

This information can be found on the P&L, financial statement, or the Dealer Operating Control (DOC). It is important to monitor this. In this example, Lube Tech's actual cost-of-sale is $18.75 per hour ($600 ÷ 32.0) for this period.

2.4 - Conversion Element #4: Expenses

How much money does it cost to operate your service department? Expenses are generally broken into three major categories:

1. Payroll Expense – all of the payroll expenses involved in operating the department.

2. Semi-Fixed or Variable Expense – these are the expenses that are directly related to the operation of the department. These include tools, unrecovered shop supplies, training costs, equipment costs, uniforms, freight, advertising, policy, and vehicle expenses.

3. Fixed Expense – this is a portion of the overall dealership expense that is allocated to the service department. This includes rent or mortgage, utilities, insurance, building repairs, taxes, and depreciation. This expense is typically allocated based on the percentage of square footage used and the percentage of payroll for the department.

These expenses can be found by reviewing the Profit & Loss (P&L) statement, operating report, or financial statement. They could also be found in an accounting expense report on your Dealer Management System (DMS).

2.5 - Conversion Element #5 – Additional Gross Profit

Additional gross profit can be derived from sublet repairs or service department revenues generated from other sources. These sources may include:

Outsourced or in-house detailing that is charged, but no labor hours flagged.

Shop supply or waste recovery fees

Revenue from other franchises moving Profit & Loss to the primary P&L

Below is an example of where you will place the Conversion information in your proforma:

Effective Labor Rate $	X	$ 125.10	2.1
MONTHLY LABOR SALES $	=	$ 212,126	
Gross Profit %	X	75.0%	2.2
LABOR GROSS PROFIT $	=	$ 159,094	
Labor Adjustments $	-	$ 3,266	2.3
Monthly Expenses $	-	$ 155,600	2.4
LABOR NET PROFIT $	=	$ 228	
Other Gross Profit $	+	$ 2,500	2.5

(Left margin label spanning the table: CONVERSION)

"Build a better world" said God, I answered "How? The world is such a vast place and so complicated now. And I am small and helpless, there's nothing I can do."

But God, in all his wisdom said "Just build a better you!"

Gordon Graham

CHAPTER 8:
Improving Profit Fundamental #2 – Conversion

2.1 - Conversion Element #1 - Effective Labor Rate

Improving the effective labor rate is, first of all, understanding the components. As described in Chapter 7, there are multiple components involved in this:

Customer Pay Effective Rate

Many service departments use op codes or different pay types to identify the components of Customer Pay Effective Rates (example: CP – Door Rate; CM – Maintenance; CC – Competitive). This provides a great resource for identifying opportunities. A process will need to be in place to ensure that advisors are using accurate pay types or op codes.

"Door Rate"is typically the highest labor rate charged. This rate is used on highly skilled and/or non-competitive repairs. For example, when a vehicle comes to you with a traction-assist or anti-lock brake problem, it is coming to you because you are the best qualified to perform these repairs, and you have an investment in training and special equipment. This operation deserves the highest labor rate. The Door Rate should be the same as the stated rate. If not, it would be an indicator that the jobs are either being discounted or the technicians are being paid for hours that are not being billed.

A best practice is to implement a Customer Pay Labor Rate document for all advisors to sign. This document would describe how and why a job would be discounted. This is intended to reduce discounting by offering other alternatives (payment plans, reward point credits, etc.).

Another best practice is to over-quote the repair by 10%. If the customer insists on a discount, the dealership gives them a 10% discount. If they don't ask for it, the advisor surprises the customer at pickup. This also allows room for additional parts that might be discovered during the repair process and, therefore, reduces the number of, horrible, "need more money" calls.

If you implement and manage a solid **Multi-Point Inspection** process as described in Chapter 6, Improving Productivity, you will likely see an improvement in Door Rate repairs, which will, therefore, improve the overall customer pay effective rate.

Another Door Rate "booster" could be **Grid Pricing**. The grid has a labor rate that varies, usually as hours increase. In this particular grid, the hourly rate for 1.0 hours is $140, the rate for 2.0 hours is $161.67 ($323.34 ÷ 2.0), the effective rate for 3.0 hours is $176.79, then at 4.0 hours the grid starts turning down. At 10.0 hours the grid is back to $141.06. This is called a roll-over grid. While many grids level out or get higher all of the way up, the philosophy of the roll-over grid is a sweet-spot between 2 and 5 hours. These repairs are typically highly skilled repairs that have little to no opportunity for comparative pricing. Example: ABS light is on…you are the place that can repair this. While the higher end labor jobs require a good bit of skill (8+ Hours), these are likely to get shopped more often, because of the total price to perform the repair. Most Dealer Management Systems (DMS) offer an option to use Grid Pricing.

Retail Repair Pricing Grid

	0	0.1	0.2	0.3	0.4	0.5	0.6	0.7	0.8	0.9
0	No Charge	$11.58	$23.70	$36.36	$49.55	$63.28	$77.55	$92.36	$107.70	$123.58
1	$140.00	$154.18	$168.40	$182.66	$196.94	$211.26	$233.68	$257.14	$281.64	$307.18
2	$323.34	$343.04	$363.07	$383.44	$404.14	$425.18	$446.56	$468.27	$490.31	$512.70
3	$530.38	$543.37	$556.06	$568.44	$580.53	$592.31	$603.79	$614.97	$625.84	$636.42
4	$652.74	$668.37	$683.96	$699.52	$715.05	$730.55	$746.01	$761.44	$776.83	$792.19
5	$808.36	$816.82	$824.97	$832.82	$840.37	$847.62	$854.56	$861.20	$867.54	$873.58
6	$888.38	$898.07	$907.58	$916.93	$926.11	$935.12	$943.96	$952.63	$961.14	$969.48
7	$983.53	$991.61	$999.53	$1,007.28	$1,014.87	$1,022.28	$1,029.53	$1,036.60	$1,043.52	$1,050.26
8	$1,063.55	$1,070.04	$1,076.36	$1,082.52	$1,088.51	$1,094.32	$1,107.20	$1,120.07	$1,132.95	$1,145.82
9	$1,158.70	$1,171.57	$1,184.44	$1,197.32	$1,210.19	$1,223.07	$1,235.94	$1,248.82	$1,261.69	$1,274.57
10	$1,287.44	$1,300.31	$1,313.19	$1,326.06	$1,338.94	$1,351.81	$1,364.69	$1,375.76	$1,386.81	$1,397.82
11	$1,410.64	$1,421.60	$1,432.52	$1,443.42	$1,454.28	$1,465.10	$1,475.89	$1,486.65	$1,497.37	$1,508.06
12	$1,520.74	$1,531.38	$1,541.98	$1,552.56	$1,563.09	$1,573.60	$1,584.07	$1,594.51	$1,604.92	$1,615.29
13	$1,627.81	$1,638.13	$1,648.42	$1,658.67	$1,668.89	$1,681.34	$1,693.80	$1,706.25	$1,718.71	$1,731.16
14	$1,743.62	$1,756.07	$1,768.52	$1,780.98	$1,793.43	$1,805.89	$1,818.34	$1,830.80	$1,843.25	$1,855.71
15	$1,868.16	$1,880.61	$1,893.07	$1,905.52	$1,917.98	$1,930.43	$1,942.89	$1,955.34	$1,967.80	$1,980.25

Maintenance Rate– is the average labor rate that we charge for oil changes, rotations, filters, and wiper blades. This rate would be based on the market "competitive analysis." We want to determine what these items are and price at or slightly above market price. No one expects dealerships to be the cheapest, but they do expect you to be competitive.

A best practice is to shop your competition. Does the local shop's oil change include the synthetic or semi-synthetic oil like yours does? Ask competitors about cabin filters. This will be fun!

Competitive Rate– is the mid-price operation that is based on comparative analysis. Comparative Analysis is for a service that the customer doesn't experience often, but they are generally aware of resources that they could shop. These operations include brake jobs, alignments, batteries, tires, and fluid exchanges. While many service departments include competitive rates in their maintenance rate calculations, you might better manage your overall effective rate if you separate the two.

A best practice for improving Competitive Rate may be "Field Trips and Training". When is the last time that your advisors have shopped batteries at an auto parts store? Why is it that they local brake shops advertise $199 brake jobs, yet the brake shop average ticket is $800-$900? You might be shocked if you heard what our advisors say to our customers about good, better, best options. If your manufacturer has good, better, best options, the advisors should be trained to ALWAYS HAVE THIS DISCUSSION, when talking about the items (brakes, batteries, etc.). This discussion should begin with the lower-priced option, the selling the advantages of the better and best options. Many advisors begin with the OEM, then condemn the other options. This approach reinforces the customer's perception that we are overpriced.

Warranty Effective Rate is the hourly labor rate that the manufacturer pays us for performing warranty repairs and predelivery inspections. In many states, the dealership has the option of selecting the Customer Price Index to increase the labor rate, or the dealer can submit a request for the retail rate option. Under the retail option, the manufacturer will reimburse the dealership at their verified customer pay "Door Rate" for most of their warranty repairs. This can create a substantial increase in the warranty effective rate. The process can be challenging, but there are companies that specialize in these calculations.

Internal Effective Rate should be the same policy as Customer Pay. It is a general consensus from many successful dealers and automotive groups that internal repair costs are recoverable in a used vehicle. Even at customer pay rates, the internal effective labor rate is extremely likely to be less than the customer pay effective rate. Reason: Internal operations are more likely to be maintenance or competitive rates (batteries, brakes, wipers, etc.) rather than repairs in the "Door Rate" category.

An attractive, alternative internal labor option might be a one labor rate option for all internal repairs. In this case, the internal labor rate would be equal to the overall customer pay effective rate, for all internal operations. In most dealerships, this would be a boost to the internal effective rate and not scare the used car manager with the Door Rate. This boost would result in higher oil change and competitive repair rates and reduced pricing for repair items. This makes a strong argument to the concept that a dealership mostly recovers reconditioning expenses. The services that would see a slight increase would be items like tires, brakes, etc. Many of these items could be noted in the appraisal process and the value of the vehicle could be adjusted accordingly.

2.2- Conversion Element #2: Gross Profit %

There are basically two ways to improve Gross Profit %, either raise Overall Effective Rate or lower Cost-of-Sale. In 2.1 – Effective Labor Rate, we discussed methods of improving Effective Labor Rate which will improve Gross Profit % assuming that the cost-of -sale remains constant or increases less than the effective rate increase. Here is some math that will assist in obtaining and maintaining the Gross Profit percentage needed for your service department.

Calculating Desired Door Rate

Determine your desired gross profit percentage. Most manufacturers have a benchmark of 72-76%. Use the following calculations to determine the optimum "Repair Door Rate" for your dealership.

- Weighted cost-of-sale (from Chapter 7, 2.2) $25.18

- Desired Gross Profit % 75.0%

Calculate the Desired Customer Pay Effective Rate to net 75% GP:

Cost-of-Sale (Weighted)		Desired Gross Profit %			Desired Cost-of-Sale %		Desired Overall Effective Rate
$25.18	÷	(100% -	75.0%	) =	25.0%	=	$100.72

Determine your work mix (Maintenance/Competitive versus Repair in hours) and Maintenance/Competitive Effective Rate; we can use the following formula to calculate our required Door Rate. If you use separate op codes or separate pay types, you could run an op code report in your DMS to find this information. Otherwise, you could grab a couple of hundred repair orders and perform an RO survey. In this case:

- Maintenance / Competitive Effective Rate $79.90

- % of Customer Pay Maintenance/Competitive: 42.0%

- % of Customer Pay Repair: 58.0%

The calculation is as follows:

Maintenance / Competitive Effective Rate*		Maintenance / Competitive Work Mix * (% of Total CP Hours)		Weighted Maintenance $ Value
$79.90	X	42.0%	=	$33.56

Desired Overall Effective Rate		Weighted Maintenance $ Value		Weighted Door Rate $ Value
$100.72	-	$33.56	=	$67.16

Weighted Door Rate $ Value		Repair / Door Rate Work Mix %		Door Rate Required
$67.16	÷	58.0%	=	$115.80

* From DMS Op Code Report or RO Survey

Controlling Cost of Sale

In Chapter 6, Section 1.5, we discussed the Technician Skill Summary and the Current Demand. This tool can be extremely valuable in determining whether we are over-skilled or under-skilled.

Over-skilled would indicate that some of our technicians are over-qualified to perform the operations that they are performing. While this might be a nice problem to have, it could also be an indicator that we might be over-paying for these operations. If you are fortunate enough to have this problem, does it mean you should send technicians packing because they are over-skilled? Heck no! This might be a great opportunity for cross-pollination.

Do we need to add repair work to our mix? Remember, repair work has a higher effective rate. Let's take a look at our inspection process. What are we recommending and selling? Refer to Chapter 6 – 1.4 for ideas on improving the process. When the inspection process is left to the technician's interpretation, some techs tend to only recommend the "gravy" items, which are likely lower-cost-competitive, or maintenance items. Other techs tend to "rubber stamp" the inspection, rather than actually performing the inspection.

Implement Production Objectives, as described in Chapter 6 – 1.4. Generally, the highest performing technicians have the highest rate-of-pay. Through their skills, training and repetition, they have learned to be very efficient. As a result, when we agree on Production Objectives, these technicians usually earn a 5% or 10% increase over their current production. This increase is likely achieved by reducing the "utilization roadblocks", that cause the technician to wait on parts, approvals, information, etc. The middle and lower productivity tier of technicians will typically agree to a 10% or 15% increase over their current production. This increase is achieved by not only reducing the "utilization roadblocks" but improving efficiency by a better focus on dispatching to the correct skill. This will lower cost of sale and therefore improve Gross Profit %. Below is an example of implementing Production Objectives. In this case, the 5/10/15% rule results in a 7.2 hours-per-day increase in productivity, while lowering cost-of-sale by .20 per hour.

					Current Situation				After Production Objectives		
Technician Name	Rate	Days Worked	Hours Flagged	Average Flagged Hours per Day	% of Total Hours	Contribution	Productivity %		Increase %	Objective	% of Total Hours	Contribution
Billy	$ 28.00	60	552.0	9.2	13%	$3.69	115%		5%	9.6	12%	$3.49
Fred	$ 30.00	58	481.4	8.3	12%	$3.57	104%		5%	8.7	11%	$3.39
Ralph	$ 30.00	60	528.0	8.8	13%	$3.79	110%		5%	9.2	12%	$3.59
Lucy	$ 24.00	56	431.2	7.7	11%	$2.65	96%		10%	8.5	11%	$2.65
Jimmy	$ 30.00	59	469.6	8.0	11%	$3.42	99%		10%	8.8	11%	$3.42
Suzy	$ 22.00	60	446.4	7.4	11%	$2.35	93%		10%	8.2	11%	$2.36
Freddie	$ 22.00	55	390.5	7.1	10%	$2.24	89%		15%	8.3	11%	$2.37
Bubba	$ 20.00	60	451.2	7.5	11%	$2.16	94%		15%	8.7	11%	$2.27
Lubi	$ 16.00	57	324.9	5.7	8%	$1.31	71%		15%	6.9	9%	$1.44
		525	4075.2	69.7	100%	$ 25.18				76.9	100%	$24.98
						Current Cost-of-Sale				+7.2 hours per day		New Cost-of-Sale

In addition, if your service department is over-skilled, you certainly will want to consider this as you hire additional technicians. Focus more on B or C level technicians to reduce the overall average cost of sale. You could likely offset some of your lost gross profit with reduced training expense.

Under-skilledtechnician staff would be an indicator that we might have: a) excess carry-overs and cycle times (vehicles waiting for a skilled tech to become available); b) poor work quality (vehicles given to an under-qualified technician with the risk of not being repaired properly); and/or c) idle, under-utilized technicians (scheduling and shop loading focused on the number of vehicles or hours, resulting in skill misbalance).

Cross Pollination

"Clean the ticket." The perfect situation for improving cycle time. Many specialized skills shops report cycle times of 1 to 3 days for repair items, not including the initial wait time. This could mean that after a week or more of appointment time, there is another day for the vehicle to enter the shop, then 3 to 9 days to complete the 3 – relatively minor repairs. Imagine the loaner car expense. Imagine the image of inconvenience that this portrays to the customer.

The solution to this challenge is the ability to clean the ticket. This is a situation where a technician, or technicians, have all the skills to efficiently perform most repairs on any vehicle in the model line without having to move the vehicle. Cycle time is reduced as most vehicles can be completed in one trip to the shop. When we are attempting to maintain balance in the cost of sale, training expense, and productivity, this is a huge accomplishment!

Cross Pollination is cross-training, in-house. We call it cross-pollination because it's different than traditional training. In a traditional training situation we have a trainer and a trainee, high-skilled, low-skilled In the cross-pollination concept, much like plants that naturally evolve due to the winds of pollination, we can intermix the skills of multiple technicians, somewhat-skilled, somewhat-skilled.

Cross Pollination Using Two-Person Teams

The Two Person Team generally incorporates a blend of skill mix as it relates to the type of repairs being performed. Originally used for quick service teams, this concept has been adopted into the mainstream. The team members provide cross-pollination in skills due to the blend. Two-person teams generally have a better lifespan than larger teams, as it is relatively easy for two people to create a partnership that mixes teamwork with a bit of competitiveness. These two people will seek out each other's strengths and use these strengths to improve productivity.

Two Person Teams require a bit of creativeness on everyone's part. This is where the fun begins! The perfect reasoning and balance in a Two Person Team might be any of the following:

- Different skill-sets to reduce cycle or duration time by a) cleaning the ticket, or b) double up on one job to share skills, knowledge and efficiency

- Youth versus Knowledge – for heavy work like engines, sometimes, a young strong technician paired with a seasoned veteran is a nice balance

- Boomers & Zoomers or X's & Z's – This is known as reverse mentoring. A Gen Z can typically pick up and use any type of electronic from the age of about 5. This generation usually understands technology much easier that their older colleagues. Whether the challenge be the technology of the vehicles or the technology of the process (computer usage, 3-C stories, or other), this could be a great assistance to technology-challenged journeyman technicians.

- The Buddy System – This is a situation where two technicians of fairly even skills are close friends and a little competitive with one another. In this system, the "buddies" push each other to constantly achieve new goals.

This next graph is an example of two technician's skills:

Ratings: 2.0 - Fully Qualified. 1.0 - Partially Qualified. 0.0 - Non Qualified	Electrical	Infotainment	Drivability	Climate Control	Brake Repair	Steering and Suspension	Engine Repair	Manual Transmission	Automatic Transmission	Diesel Engine	TOTAL SKILL POINTS
TECHNICIAN NAME											
Jimmy	1	1	0	0	1	0	2	2	2	2	11
Suzy	1	2	1	1	2	1	1	0	0	0	9

In this example, as a team, Jimmy and Suzy would be adequately skilled to perform almost any needed repair. This team could be scheduled for any type of work. While this team might be challenged, on occasion, in complicated drivability and climate control, the challenge should be minor. Another thing to look at is some technicians struggle with the entire administrative process. The two-tech team could not only cross-pollinate the technical skills, but the soft-skills as well. Some techs are much better at the administrative side (estimates, approvals, stories, flagging, etc.)

WEIGHTED COST-OF-SALE CALCULATION BASED ON PRODUCTIVITY

	Technician Name	Hourly Rate	Average Hours Flagged	Pay	% of Total Hours Flagged		Contribution
21	Jimmy	$ 30.00	45.0	$ 1,350.00	55%	=	$ 16.46
22	Suzy	$ 24.00	37.0	$ 888.00	45%	=	$ 10.83
		Total Hours	82.0	$ 2,238.00	Weighted Cost of Sale		$ 27.29

Two-Person Team Compensation

Team members will be paid based on clocked hours X hourly rate X productivity percentage.

Team Plan with Production Objective likely to see 15%+ increase in Productivity:

Current Productivity (82.0 divided by 80.0 clock) = 102.5%

Add 15.0%

New Productivity = 117.5%

Jimmy's new rate is $31.00 – ($1.00 increase for leadership role).

Suzy's rate remains at $24.00.

CALCULATE COST-OF-SALE IN TEAM PAY PLAN

Hours Produced   94.0

Technician	Hours Worked	% of Total	Pay Rate	Productivity %	Pay $
Jimmy	40.0	50.0%	$ 31.00	117.5%	$ 1,457.00
Suzy	40.0	50.0%	$ 24.00	117.5%	$ 1,128.00
				117.5%	$ -
				117.5%	$ -
	80.0	100.0%			$ 2,585.00
				Cost-of-Sale	$ 27.50

While this example increases the cost-of-sale by 0.21, the benefits far outweigh as the weekly labor sales would be increased by $1500. (@$125 effective rate) for this one team. Imagine multiplying these times 3,4,5 or 10 teams? The good news is that teams blend with other configurations whether it be dispatch or groups/teams.

Controlling the Cost of Sale by Work Mix

Many dealerships use this method to control cost-of-sale and to incentivize technicians who perform the high-skilled, high-labor-rate repairs. In Example 1, the technician might have a 2-level pay rate based on customer pay and warranty.

Example 1: Customer Pay / Warranty Variable Rates

We all likely have heard the grumbling about warranty hours being considerably less than customer pay hours. In today's world, and with most states having the Retail Warranty Rate option, many dealerships use the higher warranty effective rate to help offset some of these concerns.

2-Level Pay Plan for Retail Option Warranty Dealerships

CP Overall Effective Labor Rate		Desired CP Gross Profit %			Desired Cost-of-Sale	Average Cost-per-Hour
$100.72	X	(100 % -	75.0%	)=	25.0%	$25.18
Warranty Labor Rate		Desired Warranty Gross Profit %			Desired Cost-of-Sale	Average Cost-per-Hour
$135.00	X	(100 % -	75.0%	)=	25.0%	$33.75

In this example, the 75% desired gross profit would stage the weighted average hourly rate for all Customer Pay (and/or Internal) at $25.18 per hour and $33.75 for the warranty repairs. This reflects a 34% higher rate for warranty repairs, which is pretty close to the typical customer pay to warranty labor operation hours.

Example 2: Three-Level Pay Rates

In this example, the desired 75% gross profit would set the weighted average hourly rate for Maintenance & Competitive Services at $21.50 per hour, $31.25 for Door Rate Repairs customer-pay repairs, and $33.75 for warranty repairs. As long as cost-weighting and the labor pricing policy are adhered to, the desired gross profit will be achieved.

3-Level Pay Plan (Maintenance/Repair/Warranty)

CP Maintenance Effective Labor Rate		Desired Maintenance Gross Profit %			Desired Cost-of-Sale	Average Cost-per-Hour
$86.00	X	(100 % -	75.0%	)=	25.0%	$21.50
CP Repair Effective Labor Rate		Desired CP Repair Gross Profit %			Desired Cost-of-Sale	Average Cost-per-Hour
$125.00	X	(100 % -	75.0%	)=	25.0%	$31.25
Warranty Labor Rate		Desired Warranty Gross Profit %			Desired Cost-of-Sale	Average Cost-per-Hour
$135.00	X	(100 % -	75.0%	)=	25.0%	$33.75

Read more about pay plans in "**Chapter 12.**"

2.3 - Conversion Element #3 – Labor Adjustments

Adjustments / Unapplied Time are the adjustments made to labor gross profit due to what is called Unapplied Time. Adjustments to this account are typically performed by the payroll department as they reconcile technician payroll. It is normally a negative adjustment. Essentially, every time we close a repair order, the cost of the technician labor that we recorded is credited to the payroll account. When the payroll department completes the payroll functions, it will post a debit to that account. The payroll department then reconciles the difference into unapplied time.

The unapplied time difference is caused when we pay a technician a different amount than our repair order costs. It is important that we periodically check to make sure that the rate in our DMS's technician setup is the same as what we are actually paying them. In addition, if we pay technician hours that are not costed in the RO, it will create an adjustment. Another big adjustment can occur when we have hourly technicians. Example:

- Lube Tech makes $15.00 per hour, 40 hours per week ($15.00 x 40 = $600 per week).
- Lube Tech produces 32.0 hours for the week and is costed at $15.00 per hour ($15.00 x 32 = $480).
- $600 - $480 = $120 unapplied time.

In this case, we have a weekly unapplied time adjustment of $120. That's about $500 per month for one technician. Imagine if you have five of these technicians!

For Quick-Lube Technicians, a two-person team with a production objective and perhaps an incentive works very well to help reduce the unapplied time. It is possible for a two-person Lube Team to produce 16 hours per day if they have enough work. At 0.7 per quick-lube repair order, that is 23 oil changes per day. They should be trained on the inspection process, filter replacements, and minor recalls.

A few years ago, I was involved in an oil change study conducted by one of the manufacturers. In this study, we visited 150 dealerships for other business. Without the dealership's initial knowledge, we timed two events at each of the 150 service departments. The events were an oil and filter change, tire rotation, and inspection. We timed the total event "cycle time" and the "rack time". The majority of these events (88%) were being performed by a single technician.

The **total cycle time** (customer in to customer out) averaged 82 minutes (1 hour, 22 minutes), which was very disappointing.

The **total rack time** was the actual time that it took to perform the "event" (oil and filter change, tire rotation, and inspection). This averaged 21 minutes. This was not a hurried 21 minutes! Many of these services involved technicians talking on their phones and taking brief coffee or smoke breaks. The best "rack time" events were typically between 16 and 18 minutes.

The lessons learned from this study were:

1, An oil change, rotation, and inspection required less than 0.4 of actual technician time. The typical flag is 0.7-0.8. Can a lube tech be 100% productive? Yes.

2. Why does the dealership process require, on average, an additional 60 minutes to complete? Research shows that there is a very high closing rate for additional items (inspection) if presented within the first 25 minutes of the write-up. This closing rate diminishes rapidly after 25 minutes.

Creating a process and improving this cycle time can save a lot of gross profit in labor adjustments, not to mention improved labor sales and customer retention.

2.4 - Conversion Element #4 – Expenses

Expenses are typically designated into three main areas: personnel, semi-fixed (or variable), and fixed expense. NADA, most manufacturers, and 20 Groups offer guidelines for gross profits and expenses. These are called "Benchmarks." Benchmarks are typically the average of the top-performing dealers. We will discuss options for using Benchmarks in more detail, in Chapter 9 – Benchmarks and Reverse Engineering Your Service Department. Here is a very valuable calculation. When determining the breakeven for adding an expense, use the following calculation:

Let's say that we are considering adding a parts runner. $2600 per month plus 30% taxes, benefits = total expense of $3380.

BREAKEVEN CALCULATOR

Amount of Expense		Gross Profit %		Additional Labor Sales $	To Net
$ 3,380	÷	75.0%	=	$ 4,507	Breakeven
*Additional Labor to Net 10%		65.0%	=	$ 5,200	10%
*Additional Labor to Net 20%		55.0%	=	$ 6,145	20%

Additional Labor Sales $		Effective Labor Rate $		Additional Flat Rate Hours Required	
$ 4,507	÷	$ 100.72	=	44.7	per month
$ 5,200	÷	$ 100.72	=	51.6	per month
$ 6,145	÷	$ 100.72	=	61.0	per month

If the service department is going to pay for this person, it will require an additional 44.7 flat-rate-hours per-month to retire this expense. Since we really don't work to break-even, the calculator indicates the hours required to net 10% (51.6) or 20% (61.0) per month. To take this a step further, with 12 technicians, this will require the technicians to produce .18 to .24 additional hours per day (.2-.3) to retire or net 10-20% on this new process.

Additional Flat Rate Hours Required		Number of Technicians		# Days Worked in Month	Additional Hours per Tech/per Day
44.7	÷	12	÷	21.25	0.18
51.6	÷	12	÷	21.25	0.20
61.0	÷	12	÷	21.25	0.24

If we are confident that this new position would cause us to exceed 2.1 additional hours per day, or 0.18 per technician, it might make sense. If we want to take it a step further, let's a calculation for parts (*based on average parts to labor ratio and service parts GP):

Labor Increase Parts to Labor Ratio*

$4507 Labor Sales x 1-1 ratio= $4507.

$4507 Parts Sales x .45 Gross Profit = $2,028 Added Parts Gross

So, if this is your dealership, it probably would not be fair to your parts manager to pay $3380 for $2028 gross, but a split might work. And remember, this is a breakeven case; we certainly should far exceed this in real life. Warning: This change, as well as any other change, requires a level of management intervention. This new-hire will require a specific job description to ensure that they perform the functions defined. Otherwise, they may just become a go-fer. Also, it will require a commitment from the technicians to increase their performance level accordingly (production objectives).

This Breakeven Calculator tool can be used for calculating the purchase of a new piece of equipment, adding staff, or retiring any expense that is production-related.

Personnel Expense includes the compensation paid to the service department, non-technician employees, including managers, advisors, warranty administrators, porters, and others. Personnel may also include percentages of the compensation of dealers, general managers, and/or accounting personnel expense.

Ideas to reduce personnel expenses:

- Verify that each position is needed.

- NADA and manufacturer's guidelines recommend a technician to support ratio of 1.5-2.0 technician to staff ratio. This would suggest that a dealership with 10 technicians should have between 5.0 and 6.7 support staff. Support staff would include: managers, advisors, warranty administrators, porters, cashiers and other support employees.

  - Could Shop Foreman role be productive and provide billed hours?

  - Are Shop Foreman and/or Dispatcher positions needed? Write a Job Description for these positions, indicating exactly what they will do? What are the expected results? How will we measure them? If you cannot measure the direct results, it may raise a red flag.

  - Are Shop Foreman and/or Dispatcher positions compensation related to driving productivity in a fair and balanced way?

In the evolution of service departments, the shop foreman position was originated to help clear up the quality of work that the dispatcher was causing by "gunslinging."

- Is your advisor-to-technician ratio within range? The typical range is 3 to 4 technicians for each advisor. (3 x 8.0 hours = 24.0 hours per day, ÷ 2.2 hours per RO (Customer Pay and Warranty) = 11 customers per day.) Most manufacturers suggest and/or recommend that the advisor close out 10 to 15 customers per day.

- If we have production-focused hourly employees (vehicle staging, parts shop delivery, etc.), are we managing their processes to ensure that we are receiving the benefits on which we are focused?

Semi-fixed expenses are expenses that are incurred directly as a result of repairing and servicing vehicles. These expenses include tools, equipment, cleaning and shop supplies, uniforms, advertising, and policy adjustments.

Ideas to reduce semi-fixed expenses:

- The can-for-can shop supply policy that we discussed in Chapter 1. In this example, the technician turns an empty can of brake cleaner, lubricant, etc., in order to get a new can. This does a reasonable job of assuring that the technicians are not taking shop supplies home.

Service departments using groups or teams sometimes allocate a budget for shop supplies based on the hours produced. For example:

- The group has a 560-hour per month objective.
  - A budget of $0.25 per hour for shop supplies equals $140 per month.
  - The parts department runs a monthly invoice for each group.
  - Potential incentive for saving money.

- Special tools should be under lock and key with quick access. Either the shop foreman (if applicable) or another supervisor should inventory and control these tools or get the parts department to inventory these tools in a separate source.

While this concept usually receives pushback from the parts manager, once they realize the impact that this can have on productivity, which generates parts sales, they might be more accepting.

- Uniforms, mats, and shop rags require a lot of attention. Allowing the uniform company to count alone is a license to steal. If you do not have the resources to count with the driver, pay attention to the following things:

  A) Use shop rag auto replenishment, perform a rag count with the driver to determine the shortage, then agree on replenishment.

  B) Upon departure, from dealership, have technicians bring all uniforms to you. Create a form signed by the employee and you (or designee), along with an exit interview. If not, it seems that all technicians keep uniforms, and you pay retail for them. At least that's what the driver would like you to believe.

  C) Designate two people to be the designees to sign the weekly invoice. Notify the uniform company, in writing, of the designees and that no one else will be authorized to sign their invoices. When we allow anyone to sign the invoice, we leave ourselves open to the uniform company carpeting our shop with rental floor mats and/or signing a new contract without realizing it.

- Loaner cars are, many times, a crutch for poor productivity and scheduling. A simple means of determining this is: a) determine what percentage of your customers are in loaner cars; then b) determine how many days a customer stays in a loaner car versus a customer who is not. Reducing loaner car usage can lead to significant expense reduction.

- Policy Adjustment is typically used when a mistake happens. Unfortunately, mistakes happen. The primary method for reducing mistakes is to understand the cause in the first place. If the technician made the mistake, why? Is it lack of training? Sloppiness? If it is sloppiness or failure to pay attention, is the technician participating in the policy? How often does the same mistake repeat itself? Was it caused by a poor description or information from the advisor? Many dealerships track policy by technician and advisor. This is a great tool for monthly counseling and/or Performance Reviews. Communication - It is important for everyone to understand that no one is exempt from policy but how does each technician or advisor perform as compared to their peers?

- Aged open repair orders can be haunted. There is a saying: "Only whiskey and wine get better with time; aged repair orders stink!"It is extremely important that we, as managers, pay close attention to open repair orders, especially as they get two weeks or older. Unless the vehicle is actually in the shop waiting for parts or something, all efforts must be put into closing the RO. If there is an open repair order with parts or labor on it, and the vehicle is not there, you probably have a hit coming to policy. The key to minimizing this is to focus on not letting this happen. Many times, this is a great job for warranty administrators.

Fixed Expenses are overall dealership expenses that are allocated to the departments based on square footage, employee count, payroll amount, and/or other factors. These expenses include rent or mortgage, taxes, utilities, insurance, etc. While fixed expenses are generally not under your control, you can help lower them by being a good citizen. Good citizen responsibilities include:

- Making sure that lights, heaters, air compressors, etc., are turned off at night.

- Note to other department managers if you see utilities left on after closing.

- Train safety on a regular basis; look out for dangers. Consider spending 5 minutes at one morning huddle per week. If you Google: "automotive service department safety", you'll find hundreds of short subjects. This will help keep insurance costs at bay and your insurance carrier will love you.

2.5 - Leading Element #5: Additional Gross Profit

Additional Gross Profit is typically derived from one or more of the following:

- Non-warranty Sublet – Whether it be towing, trim repair, dent removal or other types of outsourced repairs, it is typical to add a markup. This is to offset time and expenses incurred by dealership in processing the sublet transaction. The typical rate is 15%-25%. If you sublet a lot of retail towing may want to ask your towing provider to give you a net discount.

- Detailing – When using an outside source for detail, it is best practice to mark up and/or have the detail company provide a net % discount. Even though a lot of this work might be internal (new and used cars), rarely does the service department not have a role in this process. The typical markup might be 25% to 50%.

- Shop Supplies / Waste Recovery Fees – If your state allows it, many dealerships charge a Shop Supply or Waste Recovery Fee - This fee is designed to offset the expense that the service department incurs in lubricants, cloths, cleaners, and other items that are not totally consumed in one particular repair. Some dealers credit these fees directly to the Shop Supply expense account, while others use the Shop Supplies Sales line to report the sales and cost of sale.

- Revenue from Other Sources – Many dealers that have revenue from other small-volume franchises may report their overall service operation sales and gross profit on this line.

CHAPTER 9:
Using the Proforma and Benchmarks to Reverse Engineer Your Service Business

I recall that many times I would meet someone, and they would ask me what kind of business I was in. When I responded that I worked in an auto dealership, the usual response was "Are you a car salesman?" When I replied, No, the next question was "Are you a mechanic?"I always believed this to be funny, as it appeared that very few people realized the number of positions that it requires to operate a dealership.

I love this perceived simplicity because, while the service business process is relatively simple, there are a lot of moving parts that we can either ignore or look at each part for improvement opportunities. This is what the Profit Fundamentals are all about. By understanding and using these fundamentals, it is no longer necessary to "throw mud against the wall to see what sticks!" or whatever other method that we use to hope for improvement. Hope is good, but it is not a plan!

The very first step, if you haven't already done so, is to build a current or Base Case Proforma for your dealership. This Proforma should provide an understanding of why the current situation is what it is. This is the point at which we can begin to design and make logical changes to improve the situation.

As discussed in the previous chapters, we should look at each of the elements and identify areas for improvement. Look at best practices for some or all of these ideas and decide what might be the best options for your dealership.

The important thing to understand about benchmarks is that they are numbers. Numbers do not provide answers; rather, they ask questions. By comparing your numbers to the benchmarks, you should always ask yourself, Why? Maybe you have an expense that is a significantly higher or lower percentage than the benchmark. Is that good or bad? The answer is: "It's a number!" There may be a very valid reason based on your dealership's accounting practices, work-mix or any of the factors that calculate into the number.

For example, let's say that your customer pay hours per RO are at 1.9 hours per RO. Your dealer, like many others, is convinced by their 20 group that it should be 2.5 hours per RO. First of all, this calculation is an obsolete old standard, or benchmark, which has little use in todays world. New vehicle customer retention, simplified maintenance requirements, vehicle quality, and work mix all affect this number. But the number does ask a question: Why is my number what it is compared to others?

Benchmarks are typically the average of the top 10 or 20% of performers in your 20 group or in other comparative groups. The first caution, in this case, is "Top Performers". The fact that their numbers are the highest or lowest doesn't necessarily make them good and you bad. It's a number! Numbers ask questions. What is important in this lesson is to not be defensive; rather, determine why your number is what it is. Then you can either take steps to improve or substantiate why.

Let's use Customer Pay Gross Profit percentage as a better example. Your GP% is lower than the benchmark or 20 group "top performers." This information is beneficial to you in growing your business. You immediately know that either your effective labor rate is lower than that of the top performers, or your cost-of-sale is higher than that of the best performers, or a combination of the two.

Why are you lower than the top performers? Possible reasons:

- They have a higher labor rate.

  - Is this market or area driven?

  - Is there opportunity to increase our labor rate?

- Their work-mix is higher in repair. Repair has higher effective labor rate.

  - Are they working on a higher mileage vehicle? If so, how? Are we missing an opportunity to grow that part of our business?

  - Are we doing a better job of new owner retention? This will result in a lower maintenance GP %. We should be able to compare, using OEM reports.

  - Are we doing a good job of performing inspections?

- Are we selling the recommended repairs?

Is their cost-of-sale less than yours?

  - Is your unapplied time more than theirs?

  - Are your technician pay plans appropriate?

  - Do your technician skills match your work-mix?

- In-house - Many of the answers that you seek might be under your rooftop. Compare all of your advisors using the advisor summary report from DMS. Is there a significant difference in Effective Labor Rate (ELR)? If the answer is yes, determine the difference between your advisors.

- Are some advisors underselling?

- Are some advisors overselling?

- Are advisors discounting labor rates?

- Are the higher performing advisor(s) running from shiny bumpers?

		SERVICE SALES / PROFITS		CURRENT	
				BASE	
		Leading Elements			#
FUNDAMENTALS	PRODUCTION CAPACITY	Clock Hrs. Worked Daily		8.0	1.1
		Days Worked Monthly	X	22.33	1.2
		Calendar Utilization %	X	90.4%	1.3
		Productivity %	X	87.5%	1.4
		Technician Hour Value	=	141.3	
		Number of Technicians	X	12.0	1.5
		Total Hours	=	1695.7	
	CONVERSION	Effective Labor Rate $	X	$ 125.10	2.1
		MONTHLY LABOR SALES $	=	$212,126	
		Gross Profit %	X	75.0%	2.2
		LABOR GROSS PROFIT $	=	$159,094	
		Labor Adjustments $	-	$ 3,266	2.3
		Monthly Expenses $	-	$155,600	2.4
		LABOR NET PROFIT $	=	$ 228	
		Other Gross Profit $	+	$ 2,500	2.5
	RESULT	MONTHLY NET $	=	$ 2,728	
		ANNUALIZED	X	12	
		Total Annualized Service Net Profit $	=	$ 32,741	
		ANNUAL IMPROVEMENT $	=		

These means avoiding the new vehicles that only require minor maintenance.

These are just examples of questions that the numbers ask.

Based on our sample dealership, Hometown Motors, this is our Base Case Proforma. You should build a Base Case Proforma for your dealership. If your Proforma is accurate, it should reflect the sales, gross profit, and net profit of the financial statement.

As a result of this pro forma example that we have developed, the service department is averaging $228 per month in labor net profit. While other gross profit and some manufacturers' Parts Gross Transfer are not included, it is a general standard or benchmark that a healthy service department should net 10% or more in labor net profit. In this case, the monthly labor sales should be $239,385, but they are only $212,126.

CALCULATOR TO NET A PREDETERMINED NET PERCENTAGE

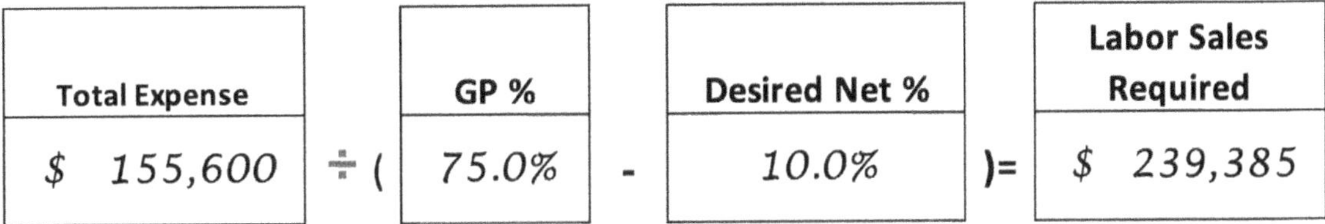

Total Expense		GP %		Desired Net %		Labor Sales Required
$ 155,600	÷ (	75.0%	-	10.0%	)=	$ 239,385

Reverse Engineering Your Proforma, is the act of determining what is the financial achievement or goal that you need to meet. This might be your dealer's "pet peeve", a 20 Group Objective or an NADA Benchmark. In this case, we will use "Net 10%". Then we apply this number to our Proforma, build the Leading Elements and create an Action Plan to accomplish these objectives.

The first step in reverse-engineering the Pro-forma would be to analyze expenses. Are there opportunities to reduce the expenses and therefore reduce the losses? In this example, we are going to say, "No." Maybe we are in a nice, relatively new dealership with great equipment, plenty of business, and just not enough production capacity.

In the sample pro forma, with the current labor sales being $212,126, we need to create an additional $27,259 in labor sales per average month in order to net 10%. This is where we begin our reverse engineering.

On the Monthly Labor Sales line of the Proforma Desired Reverse Engineered (RE) column, enter $239,385. At 10% net to sales, the Proforma calculates that the labor net profit should be $23,939 to net 10%.

Step 2. In this step, we will want to look at all of the Leading Elements above the Monthly Labor Sales line.

- Is there an opportunity to increase my effective labor rate? Using the information discussed in Chapter 8 – 2.2, maybe we should change the door rate by $10.00 per hour.

  - 50% of our work is customer pay.

  - 45% of CP is "repair," sold at Door Rate

$10.00 X 50% X 45% = $2.25 expected overall labor effective rate increase. Add $2.25 as a change to the Effective Labor Rate line on the pro forma. In addition:

- Eliminate 50% of unapplied time (estimated $1633) by managing production objectives (hourly lube technicians will now have production objectives).

- By implementing and managing production objectives, you are likely to see a minimum of 10% improvement. So, this moves your labor sales to $240,620 per month, which is not quite where you want to be, or is it?

- As a result of these actions, did your gross profit percentage change? Yes! Assuming that there are no technician pay changes, your GP% will increase due to the new Effective Labor Rate. The calculation is:

RECALCULATE GP% FOR EFFECTIVE RATE CHANGE

Current Effective Labor Rate $		(100% - Current GP %) = Cost-of-Sale %		Current Cost-of-Sale $
$ 125.10	X	25.0%	=	$ 31.28

New Effective Labor Rate $		Cost of Sale $		New Gross Profit $		New Effective Labor Rate $		New Gross Profit %
$ 127.35	-	$ 31.28	=	$ 96.08	÷	$ 127.35	=	75.4%

With these changes, this next Proforma describes the financial impact. Labor sales are up $28,494 per month, labor gross profit is up $22,334 plus the $1633 unapplied time reduction, and labor net profit has turned from $404 per month to $24,195 per month.

PROFORMA

		SERVICE SALES / PROFITS		CURRENT BASE	#	NEW SITUATION CHANGES	NEW SITUATION RESULTS	DESIRED RE
		Leading Elements			#			
FUNDAMENTALS	PRODUCTION CAPACITY	Clock Hrs. Worked Daily		8.0	1.1		8.0	
		Days Worked Monthly	X	22.33	1.2		22.33	
		Calendar Utilization %	X	90.4%	1.3		90.4%	
		Productivity %	X	87.5%	1.4	10.0%	97.5%	
		Technician Hour Value	=	141.3			157.5	
		Number of Technicians	X	12.0	1.5		12.0	
		Total Hours	=	1695.7			1889.4	
	CONVERSION	Effective Labor Rate $	X	$ 125.10	2.1	$ 2.25	$ 127.35	
		MONTHLY LABOR SALES $	=	$212,126			$240,620	$239,385
		Gross Profit %	X	75.0%	2.2	0.4%	75.4%	
		LABOR GROSS PROFIT $	=	$159,094			$181,428	
		Labor Adjustments $	-	$ 3,266	2.3	$ (1,633)	$ 1,633	
		Monthly Expenses $	-	$155,600	2.4		$155,600	
		LABOR NET PROFIT $	=	$ 228			$ 24,195	$23,939
		Other Gross Profit $	+	$ 2,500	2.5		$ 2,500	
	RESULT	MONTHLY NET $	=	$ 2,728			$ 26,695	
		ANNUALIZED	X	12			12	
		Total Annualized Service Net Profit $	=	$ 32,741			$320,335	
		ANNUAL IMPROVEMENT $	=				$287,594	

Due to the increase in gross profit and eliminating the unapplied time, you have accomplished your objective of 10% net to sales. These minor changes have resulted in an annual net profit improvement of $287,594!

This is a sample of what a pro forma can do to assist you in engineering or reverse engineering your current situation into your desired situation. In addition:

Do we have additional productivity opportunities? Even the changes that we have made only take us to 97.5% productivity. Benchmarks for technician efficiency are 125-150% for journeymen and 150-200% for master technicians. If this is true, we still have a technician utilization opportunity.

Do we have calendar utilization opportunities? Can we reduce attrition cycle time? Or can we use other ideas discussed to improve calendar utilization?

CHAPTER 10:
Building Your Playbook

Your Playbook is the owner's manual and shop manual for your service department. It is a place to store all process documents, job descriptions, and other documents that define the agreed-upon procedures for operating your service department. Recommended examples of these documents may include:

- Organization Chart(s)

- All Job Descriptions – this might be generic documents, modified to reflect dealership standards (work times, etc.), or it could be a complete detail of specific duties, such as:

- Advisor write-up process, including menu and MPI process.

- Advisor Labor Pricing Policy

- Advisor Diagnostic Sheet Process

- Warranty Administrator Claim Submission Process

- Technician Time Clocking Policy

- Technician Parts Return and Job Story Process

- Technician Vehicle Inspection Process

- Parts Procurement Procedure

- Overnight Parts Check-in and Delivery Process

- Warranty Approval Process

- Vehicle Staging Process

- Greeting and vehicle return process

- RO write-up when DMS is down.

- This list is only a sample.

When interviewing technicians to discuss productivity improvements, make notes of the roadblocks mentioned by the technicians. It's a great idea to use these notes to begin the creation of process documents for your "Playbook."

It is also a great idea to involve the appropriate staff in the preparation of each of these documents. For example, many times we, as managers, have very little knowledge of the warranty claims processing and submission procedures. Have your administrator write a detailed description that you or someone else could use to perform the job if it ever becomes necessary. Use screen prints to show the actual steps of the process. This could be amazing assistance in the event of sudden loss of staff in this position.

On the next page is a simple example of a Labor Pricing Policy Process Document. As you, the manager begins the implementation of this process, it would be recommended that we review the document with all or most of the advisors. This could very well create questions like: "What about fleet accounts that we give a lower labor rate to?"This is a GREAT question! We should talk through this, understanding the potential impact on effective rate and gross profit percentage. I have worked with many dealerships that do not give discounts to fleets, but rather over-deliver service to these customers. Some dealerships even charge a premium. Remember the old saying: "quality, cheapest, fastest" – Choose Two!

Key components of the Process Document:

- The specific expectations and/or requirements of the process.

- Means of monitoring the process.

- Agreement and signature of responsible parties.

People learn and understand in different ways. In some process documents, it might be a good idea to include a flowchart, especially if there are decisions to be made in the process.

When counseling associates in the process, the best approach is: "We agreed on this…"and "Do we need to revisit this entire process?"It's always a good idea to have the document on your desk or in your hand.

Be sure to determine and describe the method(s) that will be used to enforce each of these processes. Refer to **Chapter 2** to determine the method or methods that will be used.

This policy will outline the labor pricing policy of our dealership. The objective of this policy is to ensure everyone who generates a repair order understands without any questions, management's expectations. Our labor pricing policy is as follows:

Customer Pay Labor

The objective of our service department is to provide our customer with an outstanding service experience. Labor pricing is a key component of this objective. Our policy for labor pricing is as follows:

All labor charges with a predetermined price (i.e.: oil and filter changes, alignments etc.) will be priced according to the established and published pricing. All menu packages with a pre-established price will be charged accordingly.

All operations not found in maintenance or competitive pricing menu and do not have a pre-established labor price will priced from the current labor pricing grid (or door rate). The labor times for these operations will be found in the xxxx labor time guide. The labor amount for the time will be found on the labor pricing grid (or door rate), and this will be the labor charge to our clients.

Non-manufacturer extended service contracts will be reviewed on a <u>case by case</u> basis but should be considered "retail door".

Internal Labor

All internal labor pricing will follow the customer pay labor policy (or CP Effective Rate).

Warranty

Our warranty labor is priced according to the established OEM policy.

Discounts

The dealership will continue sending discount coupons to our service clients to simulate traffic. If the customer received the coupon in the mail, the advisory staff is authorized to extend the discount to the customer. Any other discounts require the pre-approval of the service manager.

Process Accountability

Management will monitor the progress of this process by reviewing Service Advisor Summary report from DMS, daily, weekly and monthly, to verify compliance. Management will council with team members who violate this policy. If behavior continues, discipline will escalate accordingly.

The following employees have read this policy and have evidenced their commitment to comply with this policy by placing their signature below:

_______________________   __________   ____________________

Advisor   Date   Manager

Whenever possible, design a Structured Technique that will self-police and an Operational Technique that provides audit or verification by management. In the "Pricing Policy" on the previous page, you could enforce the Structured Technique by locking or restricting the advisor's ability to discount in your DMS.

While it is always important to train and mentor new associates (in fact, we probably should create a new associate Onboarding Process Document), a Playbook Process document should be designed so that you could hand it to a new associate and they could read it and, at least, relatively understand the goals and expectations for their position.

This next example is a Technician Production Objective Process Document. This would be a tool to use when agreeing on a production objective with a technician to document the agreement made.

TECHNICIAN PRODUCTION OBJECTIVE

Technician Name _______________________ **Date** _______________

Previous Hours per Day _______________________ **Productivity %** _______________

Do these hours seem correct?

Could you do more?

What roadblocks prevent you from doing so? Can we resolve?

____

____

____

____

What will be Production Objective? [ ] Hours per Day

I committ to do my very best to accomplish this objective, once the roadblock

solutions that agreed on have been resolved.

Technician Signature ____

Date _______________________

When you hire a new associate and, on the first day(s) of hire, you discuss or train certain job requirements, the results are usually pretty positive. In fact, the results are proven to be significantly better than implementing changes with existing emplyees (old dog - new tricks). If you do not discuss or train these requirements early on, the new associate is likely to either a) determine and implement their own method of performing this activity, or b) use the advice of another associate, which wouldn't be bad if we have a well-managed process document in place for that activity.

Exceptions to Compliance – Many times I have discussed the importance of written process documents only to be confronted with questions like this: "If I tell my best-performing advisor or best-performing technician that he or she has to do this, they'll quit!" Hmmm, really?

Sometimes it is a good idea to allow exceptions. For example, several dealerships that I have spoken with have implemented a software tool to assist technicians in writing warranty stories, defining the three Cs (Concern, Cause, Correction) that the manufacturer requires. Let's face it: some of our technicians are not highly skilled at writing or typing a description of the diagnosis and work performed. In most of these dealerships, they also have technicians who are extremely good at communicating the three Cs and may push back against the requirement to use the tool. Some of these dealerships subscribe by the number of users and have set written policies that state something like the following:

- This is a tool available for your convenience, and it's use is optional, unless…

  - You have warranty chargebacks due to comments, and/or

  - You have been classified as a risk by the manufacturer (some manufacturers classify technicians that have been suspected of fraud)

  - In either of these situations, you will be required to use the tool for xx months.

The story of a Sales Meeting – This might be the best idea that I've ever gotten from a vehicle sales manager.

The dealership had a general sales training meeting every Friday morning at xx o'clock. This was a mandatory meeting for all salespersons. The dealership had about 20 salespersons, and the average salesperson sold 10 vehicles per month. The top salesperson, Terry, sold an average of 35 vehicles per month. No one else came within 20 vehicles of Terry.

As this particular meeting got started, the sales manager heard some grumbling in the back of the room and asked the group to share with the group… "This is a mandatory meeting for all, correct?", Yes, "Where is Terry?" Terry was not there.

The sales manager knew that Terry wasn't there but understood that Terry was probably out looking at the trade-ins that had come in the day before and calling prospects. Quick on his feet, the manager responded: "There is a new amendment to the requirement to attend this meeting: sell more than 30 cars per month!"

You may or may not agree with this philosophy, but it is a way. The "3-Cs" process that we discussed may be a great way of allowing exceptions, but they are clearly defined. When you implement a new, written process, it is extremely important to achieve compliance. More often than not, if your top performers understand the importance of consistency to the process, they will likely choose to comply. In the event that a part of your staff already performs this task at a high level, we probably should have them involved in the design of the required process or set the parameters for exemption.

"If you do not have a plan for the day, the day will have a plan for you."

MR. ED

CHAPTER 11:
Department Structure Options

Shop Structure is an important component in realizing the maximum productivity from our service department. There are many "ways" to align technicians and distribute the work to them on a basis that accomplishes the following objectives:

- Skill level must match to ensure that technician is competent and efficient in the service or repair.

- Availability of having repairs diagnosed and/or performed in a time agreed upon with the customer.

- Quality of work to assure that each technician has the ability to meet or exceed his or her production objectives.

We will discuss several different structures that have evolved over the years and some of the pros and cons of these structures. None are perfect at all three of the objectives mentioned, but they might be a good fit for the application. Many dealerships have modified these models to offset the challenges. We will mention some of the modifications in the structure descriptions.

The Basic Structure Model: Simple Support

The very basic service department began with a simple structure: a service manager and 3-4 technicians. The service manager meets with the customer, writes the repair order, and then dispatches the job to the most qualified technician. The manager conducts all of the communication with the customer. The manager understands the skills and production requirements of each technician. This structure was and still is the most efficient structure in every way (productivity, quality, customer satisfaction, and profitability). In modern times, this would be known as "Simple Support." The success of this structure causes growth, which will require change.

BASIC LEVEL (Level 1 - Organizational Chart and Dispatch)

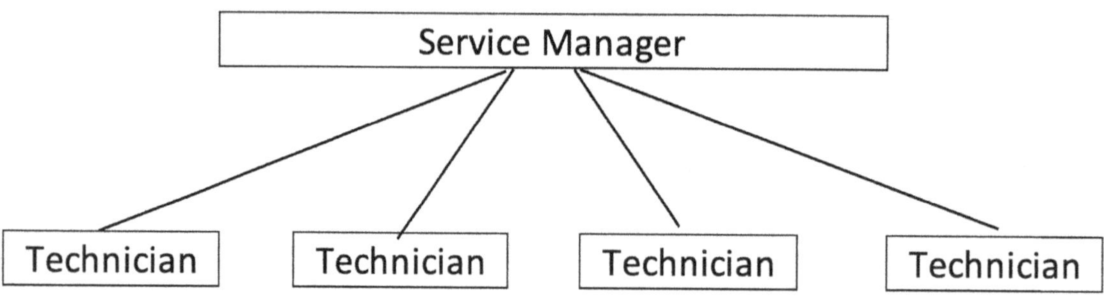

In the Level 1 structure, the Organizational Chart and Dispatch Flow are the same. Communication is awesome; the manager knows the skill levels and productivity of each technician and has made all of the commitments to the customer. The only challenge is coverage of the manager when he or she is absent.

Many times, the service department will grow into multiple Simple Support Groups. The following chart demonstrates the Organization Chart and Dispatch Flow Chart typical for a service department with 12 technicians.

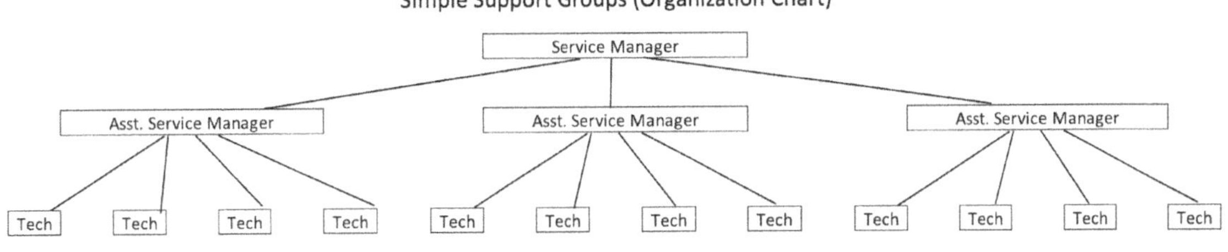

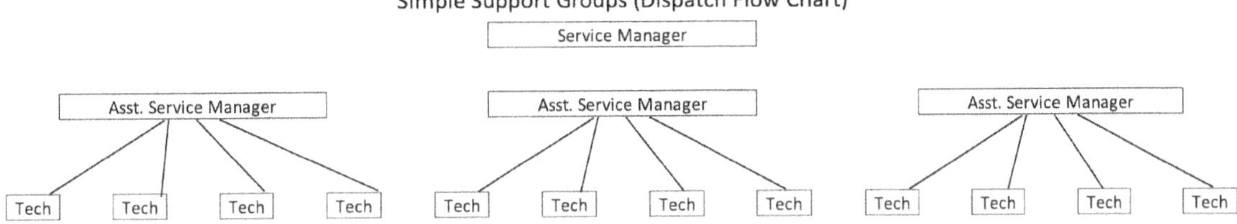

The expansion of this structure would require duplications of the service manager to create multiple Simple Support Groups. While possible, this could prove to be a challenge. How difficult would it be to duplicate the knowledge and experience that the manager possesses to multiple other "Assistant Managers"?

In addition, the challenge in the expanded Simple Support structure is three multiple lines of communication. If a customer calls in to check the status, there is a good chance (66%) that the advisor on the phone will not be able to assist them. The good news in modern times is that there are software programs available to assist with this communication challenge.

PROS: - The group structure communicates extremely well.

Very efficient process.

CONS: "Customer communication challenges."

Requires very strong (almost manager-level) advisors.

Requires strong backup coverage in the event of an advisor's absence.

Lateral Support Groups

In the Lateral Support structure, the dispatch responsibility is passed to a Group Leader. The Group Leader is a working technician who is responsible for dispatching jobs to the best-qualified person among four or more technicians, including themselves. The Group Leader receives a pay override on the production of the other technicians. This eliminates the dispatch skills required by the advisor. The Group Leader, it is very likely a highly skilled, experienced technician can understand the group's strengths and and weaknesses and dispatch accordingly.

PROS: When used with Production Objectives, very good production improvements.

- Advisor skills become very pronounced*

CONS: - Advisor position requires a backup plan (vacation, time-off coverage).

In-bound customer status calls can be confusing due to different divisions (groups).

The cost of sales or expenses is impacted by Group Leader override pay.

- Advisor skills become very pronounced*

* Depending on your perspective, advisor skills will be very pronounced. If an advisor is weak, you will be required to solve problems. This could be either good or bad, depending on your desire and resolve to correct it.

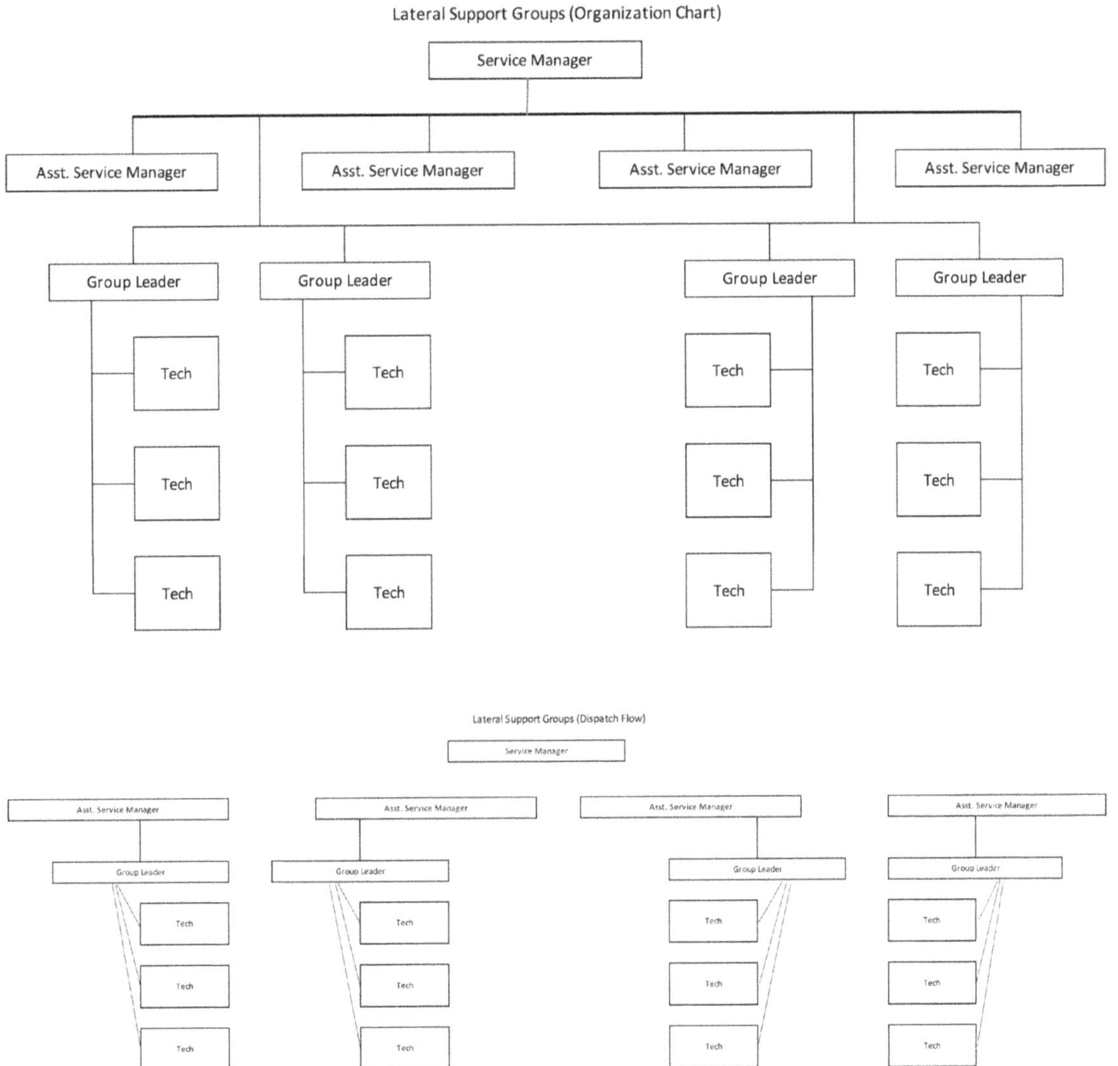

Lateral Support Super Groups

This structure enlarges the Lateral Support Group to 8-10 technicians, with a Group Leader, a Lead Technician and two Advisors. This structure creates depth that helps in the task of Advisor and Group Leader coverage, at the sacrifice of reduced communication and reduces Group Leader productivity.

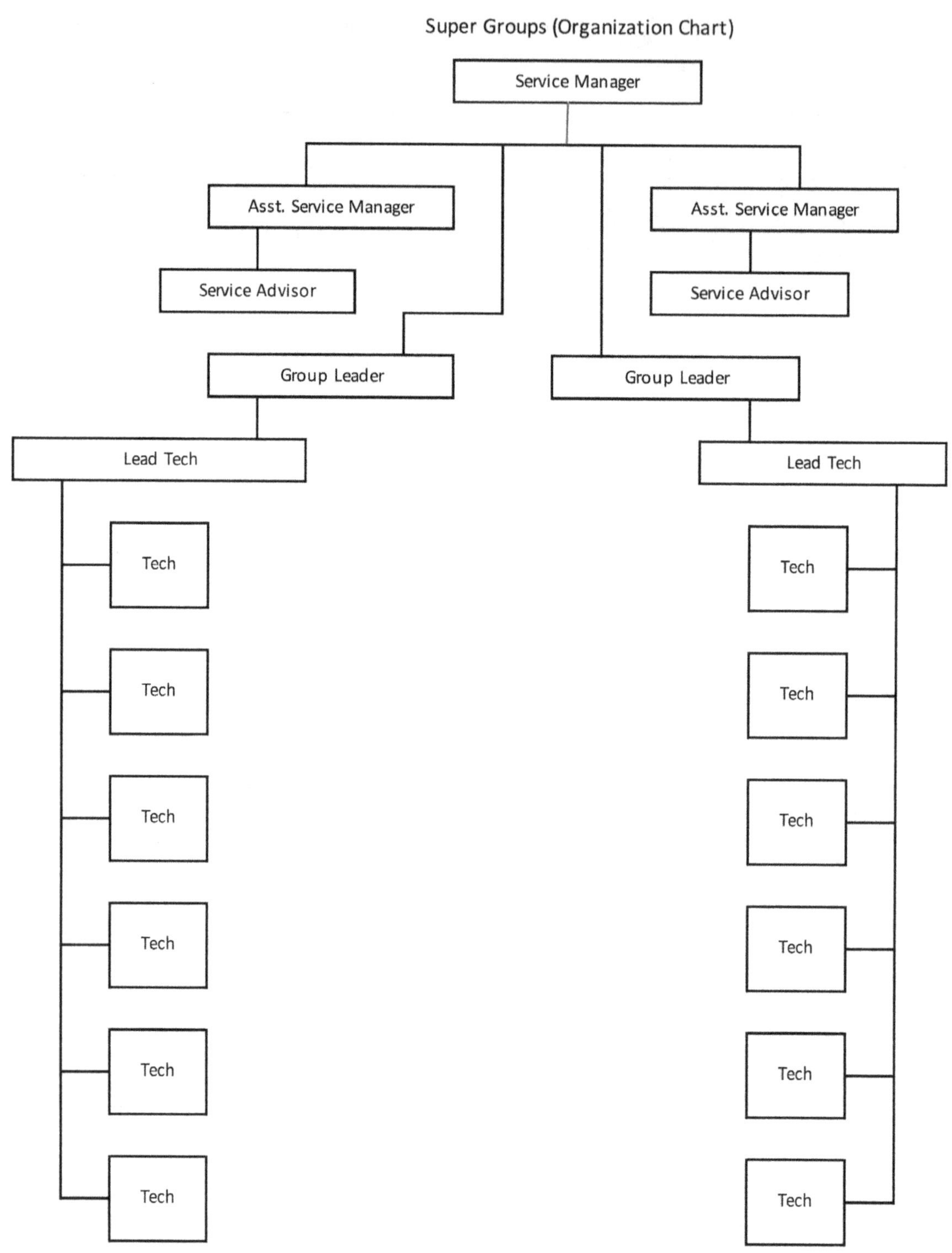

Super Groups (Organization Chart)
Service Manager
Asst. Service Manager
Asst. Service Manager
Service Advisor
Service Advisor
Group Leader
Group Leader
Lead Tech
Lead Tech
Tech
Tech
Tech
Tech
Tech
Tech
Tech
Tech
Tech
Tech
Tech
Tech

As one can see in the dispatch flow chart, the Super Group Leader spends a lot of time managing the dispatch portion of his or her job. As a result, the person who is likely the most talented in the group becomes less productive. This will demand that the Group Leader be paid a higher override on the performance of the other group members.

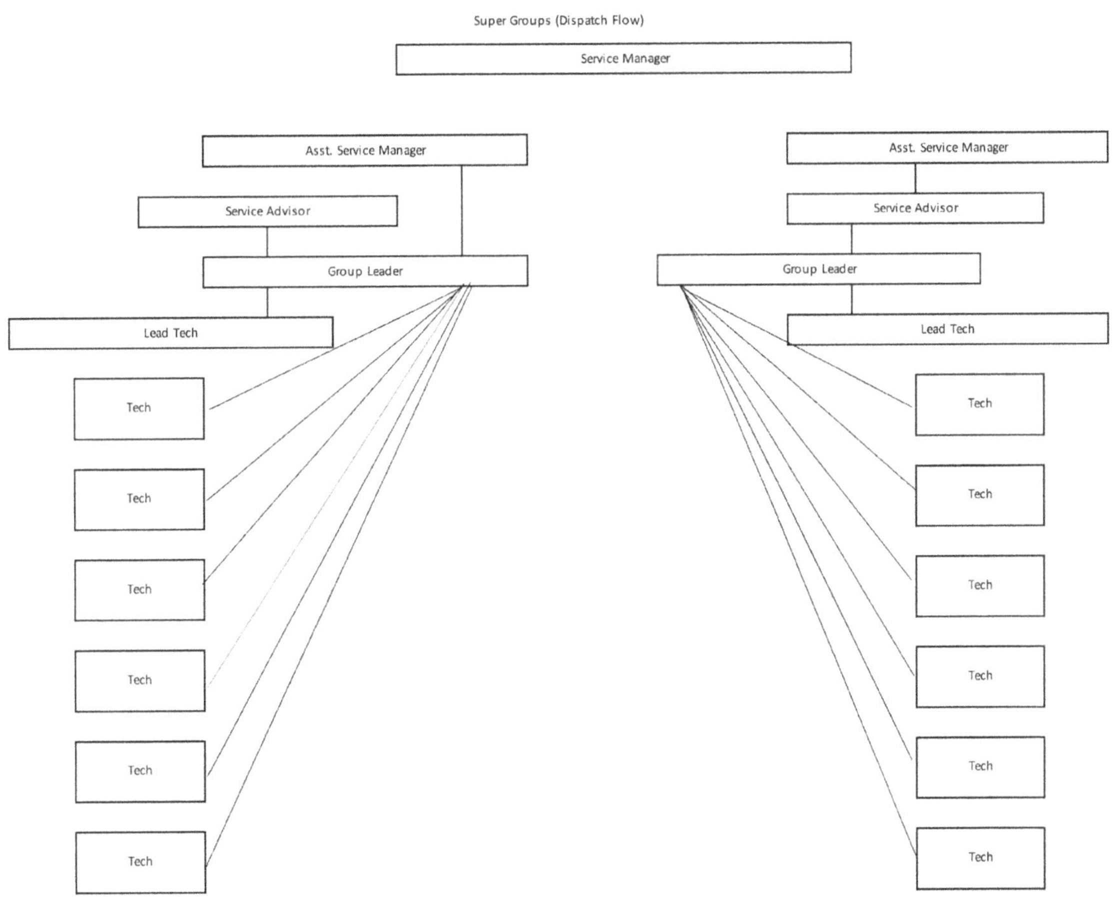

PROS: When used with Production Objectives, there are reasonably good production improvements.

-Two advisors help offset skill by one advisor.

-Two advisors make time-off coverage easier.

The Lead Technician can assist the Group Leader and cover the dispatch obligations in the Group Leader's absence.

CONS: The group leader is less productive in this structure, as it requires more of this person's time to dispatch jobs.

-Less productivity on the Group Leader's part typically requires higher pay overrides to offset.

-Two advisors help offset the potential lack of skill by one advisor.

-Multiple Super-Groups may experience customer communication challenges due to the different lines of communication.

Central Dispatch Shop

In a Central Dispatch Shop, the jobs are distributed through a central dispatch source to all of the technicians in the shop. The dispatch source might be a dispatcher, an electronic system, shop foreman, or a service manager. Using logs or electronic tools, this structure could support good customer communication as it relates to status. Depending on the size of the technician staff, this system may run the risk of being out of touch with the technicians. This may promote the "Flat Rate Mentality". Are jobs dispatched fairly? How do you know? When using electronic dispatch, it would likely be a huge mistake to leave it unattended, as most of these systems are easily manipulated by clever technicians. Plus, electronic dispatch systems pose little to no sense of urgency. Techs could go home with waiters in the customer waiting area. The system will not go grab a technician to get that job done that is overdue!

The Service Manager dispatch works the best, just like the basic service manager structure model. Once again, who understands the skills and production needs better than the manager? The huge challenge is: "Who is going to do the rest of the service manager's job?" I have seen extremely successful service manager dispatch operations in larger shops, but it involved either a dealer or general manager who was actively engaged and involved in the service department or the use of co-service managers. After all, in a larger shop, dispatching is a full-time job!

If using a dispatcher or shop foreman to conduct dispatch, the following is critical:

Each technician must have a production objective.

A high percentage of the Dispatcher/Shop Foreman's compensation must be based on individual technician meeting or exceeding production objectives. Example:

- 40% based on overall shop flagged hours
- 20% cased on CSI
- 40% based on technician meeting objective (Shop of 20 technicians = 2% of comp based on each technician meeting objective)

Without the use of these components, it is extremely difficult to overcome a perception of "dispatch unfairness" among the technicians. The perception of unfairness deflates confidence in management, which creates cultural challenges.

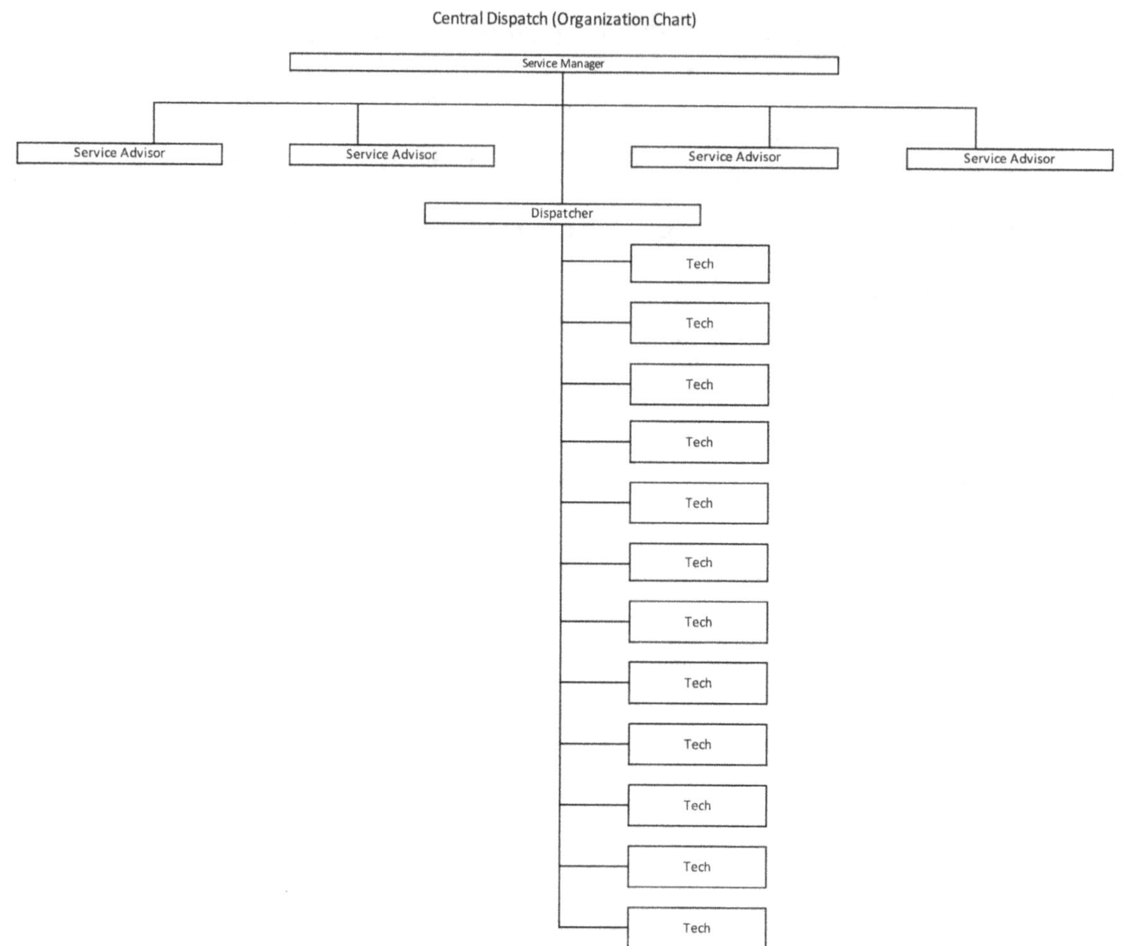

As one can see by the dispatch flow in the chart below, the dispatcher becomes a critical "kingpin" to the service department. If this person fails, the service department fails. Sometimes, this person likes to hold the shop ransom due to their power. Because every work order goes through the dispatcher, 100% coverage is essential. If the dispatcher is out for any reason, the work stops if he or she is not replaced.

Another potential negative is favoritism, or perceived favoritism, by the dispatcher. Maybe the dispatcher has some buddies, and/or maybe the dispatcher just makes sure the best techs are happy. We want every technician to be happy. This is why compensation based on each technician achieving their individual objectives is imperative.

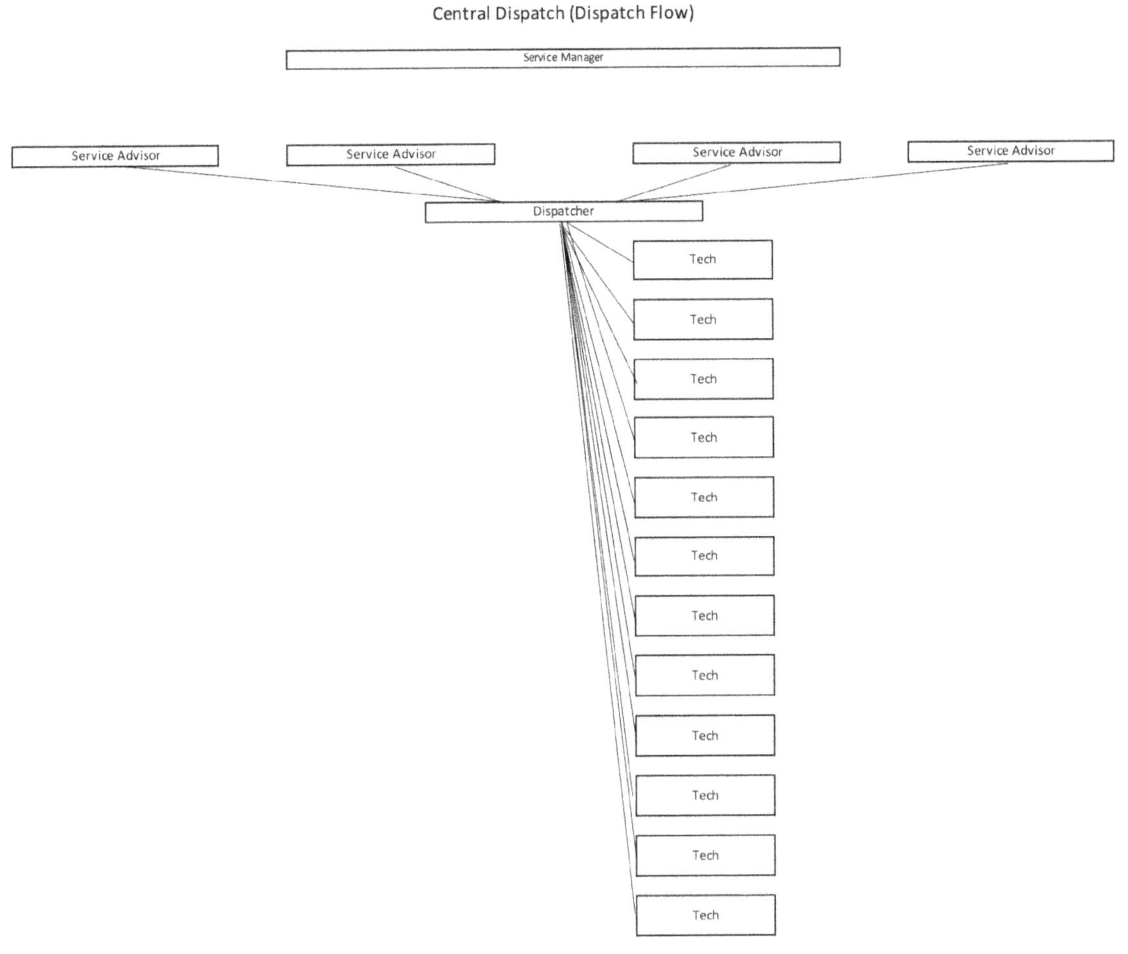

Production Teams

This structure can be the most efficient yet least understood of all structures. As the Organizational Chart indicates, the team structure looks just like the Lateral Support Structure. The difference is the way that technicians are compensated.

In this structure, the technicians are each paid based on Clock Hours Worked X Individual Pay Rate X Team Productivity %.

Team Pay Example

Hours Produced	180.4

Technician	Hours Worked	% of Total	Pay Rate	Productivity %	Pay $
Ralph	40.0	25.0%	$45.00	112.8%	$2,288.26
Jimmy	40.0	25.0%	$30.00	112.8%	$1,525.51
Suzi	40.0	25.0%	$18.00	112.8%	$915.30
Billy	40.0	25.0%	$15.00	112.8%	$762.75
	160.0	100.0%			$5,491.83
				Cost-of-Sale	$30.44

All of the hours are flagged as a team. This structure can do an amazing job of training, as a team typically has an A-Tech Team Leader, a B-Tech with fair skills, and two semi-skilled technicians. The pay plan encourages the Team Leader to double up technicians on one vehicle, which promotes skill-pollination and reduces cycle times. The B-Tech strives to become a Team Leader, and the semi-skilled strive to become B or even A technicians. Because the structure splits the hours, the Team Leader and B-Tech can be paid substantially more, per hour, than a regular flat-rate technician.

Very much like the Lateral Support Structure, the Team Leader will quickly develop an excellent knowledge of each technician's strengths and weaknesses and use that knowledge to benefit the productivity of the team.

While the team structure can work alone in shops or in combination with other structures (lateral support, etc.), teams also work really well in other variations. Examples include:

- Two-technician quick service teams will double up on maintenance and competitive operations that usually have waiting customers.

- Three-Tech paint teams use two apprentice-level sanding and masking techs and a journeyman painter who spends the majority of his or her time in the paint booth.

- Two tech cross-pollination teams operate within another structure (Dispatch, Lateral Support, or Super Groups). These two technicians work as a team, using a team pay plan, creating the ability to clean more repair orders with their skill mix. The technicians cross-train each other and/or develop "ways" to improve productivity. This structure builds a fun, competitive environment. Because of the 2-to-1 dispatch ratio, the dispatcher or group leader can reduce the dispatch load by as much as 50%. This structure would typically be optional within the department or group. Super groups might have one, two, or three teams within their group. Lateral support might have one or two teams within its group. Central Dispatch could have a variable number of two-person teams.

Hybrid Lateral Support / Teams

This is an interesting concept that is being used and may be a perfect fit in today's society. As we have discussed in other parts of the book, flexibility seems to be part of the magic in creating a friendly-for-all culture. This system blends lateral support with 2-tech teams to provide different options for different personalities and skill levels.

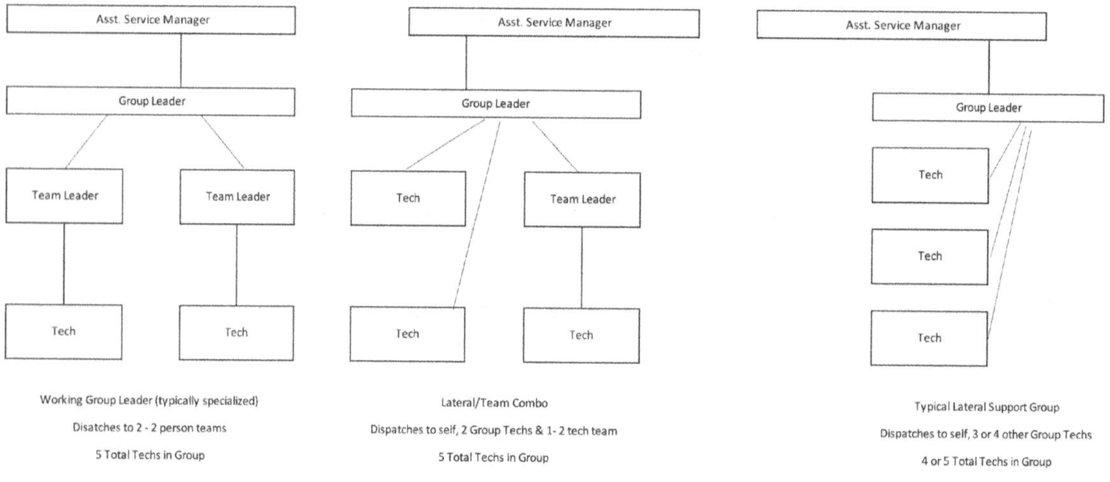

As you can see from the sample workflow chart, this shop has three groups and fourteen technicians.

Group 1 (left) utilizes a working Group Leader and two 2-tech teams. In this configuration, the Group Leader might be a specialty tech (engines and/or transmissions or other specialties). As jobs come in, the Group Leader removes the specialty jobs, then divides the remainders between the two teams. The team leaders decide how each job will be completed.

Group 2 (center) utilizes a Group Leader, two additional lateral support techs, and a 2-tech team. The Group Leader dispatches to him or herself, two lateral support technicians and the 2-tech team. Again, the team leader decides how each job will be completed.

Group 3 (right) is a pure Lateral Support Group. The Group Leader dispatches to themselves and the three or four additional techs.

Variations to Service Department Structures

Many dealerships have adopted variations of the structures that have been successful in their situations:

- Software Solutions – There are many software solutions to the communication gaps that are created by production structures, especially in communications. It is highly recommended that you study these solutions and decide on the best option.

- Mixed-structure teams and groups are very compatible. Mixtures create alternatives, which may positively stimulate culture.

- Dispatch within Structures – In this situation, all jobs are dispatched to a team or group based on the repair order number. The last digit of the RO assigns the job to a group or team of technicians. While this method takes some of the personality and accountability out of the group, it reduces the dependency on a group or team advisor to be on hand at all times. It can also help cover for weaker advisors.

When tailoring a structure for your service department, it is advised that you define the complete structure in a written process document. Even if you modify the structure midstream, you can modify the document midstream. Failure to do this can result in your team believing that all of the rules and guidelines are flexible and that they are free to change anything. While we encourage feedback, we will only change the process as a team.

"True leaders are never satisfied, always looking to improve."

"Being satisfied, invites complacency."

CHAPTER 12:
Technician Pay Options

According to a study performed by Carlisle and Company, 66% of technicians would discourage others from becoming technicians. Their primary reasons were:

- Flat rate pay leads to unpredictable income.

- Hours of unpaid work (installing tags, scanning for codes, test-driving cars, etc.).

- Discourages a healthy work-life balance.

- Length of time to reach journeyman status compared to other jobs or careers.

As we discussed in **Chapter 3** "The Flat Rate Mentality",many technicians feel that they are only independent contractors to the dealership and not really part of the team.

These challenges can be addressed in pay plans and in culture. Regardless of how we address these issues, we must manage production and stop hoping that it will manage itself! Remember, we sell time; our inventory is time, and our unsold, unused inventory becomes obsolete at the end of each day. Actively managing productivity on a daily basis helps take some of the sting out of flat rate.

According to another recent survey, 26% of technicians would prefer a flat rate with a guarantee; 34% prefer hourly with a flat-rate incentive, and 21% prefer hourly alone. Here are some options for your consideration:

Variations in Flat Rate Pay Plans

Hourly + Flat Rate

This simple pay plan combines a clock-hourly rate with a flag-hour rate. This plan works well alongside flat-rate pay as an alternative. While the Carlisle study indicated an overall poor opinion of flat-rate pay plans, 16% of the respondents actually love flat rate! Here is an example of an Hourly + Flat Rate Pay:

Technician A is currently working as a flat rate tech -$30.00 per hour.

Hourly + Flat Rate Option:

Tech A – Hourly Pay Rate (clock): $20.00 per hour

Flag Hour Rate (below objective): $10.00 per hour

Flag Hour Rate (at objective or higher): $12.00 per hour

You're likely to see slightly less productivity compared to a traditional flat-rate pay plan, but it may be a good recruiting tool. It shifts more of the Production Objective management to Operational Operating Structure.

Flat Rate with Guarantee

Variations of this type of compensation are very common in union shops. There are two flat-rate pay levels for technicians: A and B. For example:

- A-Tech: $35.00 per flat-rate hour, 35-hour guarantee.

- B-Tech: $32.00 per flat-rate hour, 35-hour guarantee.

An A-Level paid tech will move to the B-Level tech if they draw guarantee for three weeks in a row and return to A-Level after exceeding guarantee for three weeks in a row.

Team Pay Plan

The Team Pay Plan is used in conjunction with a Team Production Structure. This pay plan shares the production hours with the other members of the team. Example:

Hours Produced	180.4

Technician	Hours Worked	% of Total	Pay Rate	Productivity %	Pay $
Ralph	40.0	25.0%	$45.00	112.8%	$ 2,288.26
Jimmy	40.0	25.0%	$30.00	112.8%	$ 1,525.51
Suzi	40.0	25.0%	$18.00	112.8%	$ 915.30
Billy	40.0	25.0%	$15.00	112.8%	$ 762.75
	160.0	100.0%			$ 5,491.83
				Cost-of-Sale	$ 30.44

This pay plan may lessen the overall stress of "flat rate mentality" because the tension is spread amongst several technicians. Usually, the team leader can be paid a significantly higher hourly rate as the productivity of the lower-skilled techs are much higher. If a tech is not carrying their weight, other team members may get frustrated. Teams are usually very productive and do a great job of training.

Multi-Level Flat Rate

The Multi-Level Flat Rate plan can be used to accomplish the following:

- Help focus skilled techs on higher-effective labor rate repair work.

- Improve gross profit on Maintenance and Competitive work by having lower skilled, lower paid techs perform.

This graph demonstrates an example of having an average cost-of-sale based on your maintenance/competitive labor rate and another rate based on door rate repairs.

CP Maintenance / Competitive Effective Labor	Desired Gross Profit %	Desired Cost-of-Sale	Average Cost-per-Hour
$82.50	X (100 - 73)=	27%	$22.27
Door Rate Repair	Desired Gross Profit %	Desired Cost-of-Sale	Average Cost-per-Hour
$150.00	X (100 - 77)=	23%	$34.50

Warranty Multi-Level Flat Rate

Many states have laws that require the manufacturer to pay the dealership retail parts and labor for warranty repairs if the dealership elects the option. In the calculations, the dealership can remove maintenance and competitive items from the survey, which causes your warranty rate to be at or near your "door" rate. If you live in one of these states and you have opted for the retail option, it is likely that your warranty labor rate is substantially higher than your customer-pay effective labor rate.

Using this pay plan will do a good job of offsetting the warranty labor time stigma that our flat-rate technicians struggle with.

Take a look at an example:

2-Level Pay Plan for Retail Option Warranty Dealerships

CP Overall Effective Labor Rate		Desired CP Gross Profit %			Desired Cost-of-Sale	Average Cost-per-Hour
$100.72	X	(100 % -	75.0%	)=	25.0%	$25.18
Warranty Labor Rate		Desired Warranty Gross Profit %			Desired Cost-of-Sale	Average Cost-per-Hour
$135.00	X	(100 % -	75.0%	)=	25.0%	$33.75

This sample dealership has a warranty rate of $135.00 and a customer pay effective rate of $100.72. If we desire a 75% gross profit, we could implement a pay plan that would average $25.18 per hour on customer pay and $33.75 on warranty repairs. This is a 34% premium for warranty, which should help offset the attitude associated with the difference in the labor time allowances.

Technician Name	Average Hours Flagged	Work Mix CP %	CP Hours	Work Mix Warranty %	Warranty Hours	Level I Customer Pay Rate	Level II Warranty Pay Rate	Level I Comp	Level II Comp
Billy	46.0	47%	21.6	53%	24.4	$30.00	$37.50	$648.60	$914.25
Fred	41.5	55%	22.8	45%	18.7	$30.00	$37.50	$684.75	$700.31
Ralph	44.0	38%	16.7	62%	27.3	$30.00	$37.50	$501.60	$1,023.00
Lucy	38.5	58%	22.3	42%	16.2	$27.00	$33.50	$602.91	$541.70
Jimmy	39.8	56%	22.3	44%	17.5	$27.00	$33.50	$601.78	$586.65
Suzy	37.2	67%	24.9	33%	12.3	$24.00	$30.00	$598.18	$368.28
Freddie	35.5	66%	23.4	34%	12.1	$24.00	$30.00	$562.32	$362.10
Bubba	37.6	73%	27.4	27%	10.2	$22.00	$28.00	$603.86	$284.26
Lubi	28.5	80%	22.8	20%	5.7	$15.00	$15.00	$342.00	$85.50
	348.6		204.4		144.2			$5,145.99	$4,866.05
							Cost-of-Sale	$25.18	$33.74

This is an example of what individual pay rates might look like. The weighted cost-of-sale would be $25.18 for customer pay and $33.74 for warranty. This will accomplish the 75% gross margin that you desire, as long as the pricing policy is adhered to.

Hourly Pay Plans

The first and most important thing to remember when operating an hourly paid service department is "the sweet spot". We've discussed, for example, that if you pay an hourly quick service technician $15.00 per hour and they are 75% productive, our actual cost-of-sale is $20.00 per hour. ($15.00 ÷ .75 = $20.00) The following graph illustrates the sweet spot of 100% productivity. If the technician's productivity is 100%, their cost-of-sale is accurate. If their productivity is on the left side of the highlighted column, their cost-of-sale is higher than their pay rate. If their productivity is in a column to the right side of the highlighted column, then their cost-of-sale is lower than their actual pay rate. This can allow you to balance your cost-of-sale and avoid unapplied time. As we will detail in the first hourly option, we can actually increase hourly pay rates based on productivity while reducing the cost-of-sale. The columns represent various productivity levels, and the far-left row represents hourly pay rates. Each of the cells represents the cost-of-sale for the hourly rate row that lines up with the appropriate production percentage column.

Overall COS for Hourly Pay Rates

DAILY PRODUCTION - Flat Rate Production Hours / Production % (Based on 8.0 hour workday)

HOURLY PAY RATE	6.0 75%	6.5 81%	7.0 88%	7.5 94%	8.0 100%	8.5 106%	9.0 113%	9.5 119%	10.0 125%	10.5 131%	11.0 138%	11.5 144%	12.0 150%
$ 15.00	$ 20.00	$ 18.46	$ 17.14	$ 16.00	$ 15.00	$ 14.12	$ 13.33	$ 12.63	$ 12.00	$ 11.43	$ 10.91	$ 10.43	$ 10.00
$ 15.50	$ 20.67	$ 19.08	$ 17.71	$ 16.53	$ 15.50	$ 14.59	$ 13.78	$ 13.05	$ 12.40	$ 11.81	$ 11.27	$ 10.78	$ 10.33
$ 16.00	$ 21.33	$ 19.69	$ 18.29	$ 17.07	$ 16.00	$ 15.06	$ 14.22	$ 13.47	$ 12.80	$ 12.19	$ 11.64	$ 11.13	$ 10.67
$ 16.50	$ 22.00	$ 20.31	$ 18.86	$ 17.60	$ 16.50	$ 15.53	$ 14.67	$ 13.89	$ 13.20	$ 12.57	$ 12.00	$ 11.48	$ 11.00
$ 17.00	$ 22.67	$ 20.92	$ 19.43	$ 18.13	$ 17.00	$ 16.00	$ 15.11	$ 14.32	$ 13.60	$ 12.95	$ 12.36	$ 11.83	$ 11.33
$ 17.50	$ 23.33	$ 21.54	$ 20.00	$ 18.67	$ 17.50	$ 16.47	$ 15.56	$ 14.74	$ 14.00	$ 13.33	$ 12.73	$ 12.17	$ 11.67
$ 18.00	$ 24.00	$ 22.15	$ 20.57	$ 19.20	$ 18.00	$ 16.94	$ 16.00	$ 15.16	$ 14.40	$ 13.71	$ 13.09	$ 12.52	$ 12.00
$ 18.50	$ 24.67	$ 22.77	$ 21.14	$ 19.73	$ 18.50	$ 17.41	$ 16.44	$ 15.58	$ 14.80	$ 14.10	$ 13.45	$ 12.87	$ 12.33
$ 19.00	$ 25.33	$ 23.38	$ 21.71	$ 20.27	$ 19.00	$ 17.88	$ 16.89	$ 16.00	$ 15.20	$ 14.48	$ 13.82	$ 13.22	$ 12.67
$ 19.50	$ 26.00	$ 24.00	$ 22.29	$ 20.80	$ 19.50	$ 18.35	$ 17.33	$ 16.42	$ 15.60	$ 14.86	$ 14.18	$ 13.57	$ 13.00
$ 20.00	$ 26.67	$ 24.62	$ 22.86	$ 21.33	$ 20.00	$ 18.82	$ 17.78	$ 16.84	$ 16.00	$ 15.24	$ 14.55	$ 13.91	$ 13.33
$ 20.50	$ 27.33	$ 25.23	$ 23.43	$ 21.87	$ 20.50	$ 19.29	$ 18.22	$ 17.26	$ 16.40	$ 15.62	$ 14.91	$ 14.26	$ 13.67
$ 21.00	$ 28.00	$ 25.85	$ 24.00	$ 22.40	$ 21.00	$ 19.76	$ 18.67	$ 17.68	$ 16.80	$ 16.00	$ 15.27	$ 14.61	$ 14.00
$ 21.50	$ 28.67	$ 26.46	$ 24.57	$ 22.93	$ 21.50	$ 20.24	$ 19.11	$ 18.11	$ 17.20	$ 16.38	$ 15.64	$ 14.96	$ 14.33
$ 22.00	$ 29.33	$ 27.08	$ 25.14	$ 23.47	$ 22.00	$ 20.71	$ 19.56	$ 18.53	$ 17.60	$ 16.76	$ 16.00	$ 15.30	$ 14.67
$ 22.50	$ 30.00	$ 27.69	$ 25.71	$ 24.00	$ 22.50	$ 21.18	$ 20.00	$ 18.95	$ 18.00	$ 17.14	$ 16.36	$ 15.65	$ 15.00
$ 23.00	$ 30.67	$ 28.31	$ 26.29	$ 24.53	$ 23.00	$ 21.65	$ 20.44	$ 19.37	$ 18.40	$ 17.52	$ 16.73	$ 16.00	$ 15.33
$ 23.50	$ 31.33	$ 28.92	$ 26.86	$ 25.07	$ 23.50	$ 22.12	$ 20.89	$ 19.79	$ 18.80	$ 17.90	$ 17.09	$ 16.35	$ 15.67
$ 24.00	$ 32.00	$ 29.54	$ 27.43	$ 25.60	$ 24.00	$ 22.59	$ 21.33	$ 20.21	$ 19.20	$ 18.29	$ 17.45	$ 16.70	$ 16.00
$ 24.50	$ 32.67	$ 30.15	$ 28.00	$ 26.13	$ 24.50	$ 23.06	$ 21.78	$ 20.63	$ 19.60	$ 18.67	$ 17.82	$ 17.04	$ 16.33
$ 25.00	$ 33.33	$ 30.77	$ 28.57	$ 26.67	$ 25.00	$ 23.53	$ 22.22	$ 21.05	$ 20.00	$ 19.05	$ 18.18	$ 17.39	$ 16.67
$ 25.50	$ 34.00	$ 31.38	$ 29.14	$ 27.20	$ 25.50	$ 24.00	$ 22.67	$ 21.47	$ 20.40	$ 19.43	$ 18.55	$ 17.74	$ 17.00
$ 26.00	$ 34.67	$ 32.00	$ 29.71	$ 27.73	$ 26.00	$ 24.47	$ 23.11	$ 21.89	$ 20.80	$ 19.81	$ 18.91	$ 18.09	$ 17.33
$ 26.50	$ 35.33	$ 32.62	$ 30.29	$ 28.27	$ 26.50	$ 24.94	$ 23.56	$ 22.32	$ 21.20	$ 20.19	$ 19.27	$ 18.43	$ 17.67
$ 27.00	$ 36.00	$ 33.23	$ 30.86	$ 28.80	$ 27.00	$ 25.41	$ 24.00	$ 22.74	$ 21.60	$ 20.57	$ 19.64	$ 18.78	$ 18.00
$ 27.50	$ 36.67	$ 33.85	$ 31.43	$ 29.33	$ 27.50	$ 25.88	$ 24.44	$ 23.16	$ 22.00	$ 20.95	$ 20.00	$ 19.13	$ 18.33
$ 28.00	$ 37.33	$ 34.46	$ 32.00	$ 29.87	$ 28.00	$ 26.35	$ 24.89	$ 23.58	$ 22.40	$ 21.33	$ 20.36	$ 19.48	$ 18.67
$ 28.50	$ 38.00	$ 35.08	$ 32.57	$ 30.40	$ 28.50	$ 26.82	$ 25.33	$ 24.00	$ 22.80	$ 21.71	$ 20.73	$ 19.83	$ 19.00
$ 29.00	$ 38.67	$ 35.69	$ 33.14	$ 30.93	$ 29.00	$ 27.29	$ 25.78	$ 24.42	$ 23.20	$ 22.10	$ 21.09	$ 20.17	$ 19.33
$ 29.50	$ 39.33	$ 36.31	$ 33.71	$ 31.47	$ 29.50	$ 27.76	$ 26.22	$ 24.84	$ 23.60	$ 22.48	$ 21.45	$ 20.52	$ 19.67
$ 30.00	$ 40.00	$ 36.92	$ 34.29	$ 32.00	$ 30.00	$ 28.24	$ 26.67	$ 25.26	$ 24.00	$ 22.86	$ 21.82	$ 20.87	$ 20.00
$ 30.50	$ 40.67	$ 37.54	$ 34.86	$ 32.53	$ 30.50	$ 28.71	$ 27.11	$ 25.68	$ 24.40	$ 23.24	$ 22.18	$ 21.22	$ 20.33
$ 31.00	$ 41.33	$ 38.15	$ 35.43	$ 33.07	$ 31.00	$ 29.18	$ 27.56	$ 26.11	$ 24.80	$ 23.62	$ 22.55	$ 21.57	$ 20.67
$ 31.50	$ 42.00	$ 38.77	$ 36.00	$ 33.60	$ 31.50	$ 29.65	$ 28.00	$ 26.53	$ 25.20	$ 24.00	$ 22.91	$ 21.91	$ 21.00
$ 32.00	$ 42.67	$ 39.38	$ 36.57	$ 34.13	$ 32.00	$ 30.12	$ 28.44	$ 26.95	$ 25.60	$ 24.38	$ 23.27	$ 22.26	$ 21.33
$ 32.50	$ 43.33	$ 40.00	$ 37.14	$ 34.67	$ 32.50	$ 30.59	$ 28.89	$ 27.37	$ 26.00	$ 24.76	$ 23.64	$ 22.61	$ 21.67
$ 33.00	$ 44.00	$ 40.62	$ 37.71	$ 35.20	$ 33.00	$ 31.06	$ 29.33	$ 27.79	$ 26.40	$ 25.14	$ 24.00	$ 22.96	$ 22.00
$ 33.50	$ 44.67	$ 41.23	$ 38.29	$ 35.73	$ 33.50	$ 31.53	$ 29.78	$ 28.21	$ 26.80	$ 25.52	$ 24.36	$ 23.30	$ 22.33
$ 34.00	$ 45.33	$ 41.85	$ 38.86	$ 36.27	$ 34.00	$ 32.00	$ 30.22	$ 28.63	$ 27.20	$ 25.90	$ 24.73	$ 23.65	$ 22.67
$ 34.50	$ 46.00	$ 42.46	$ 39.43	$ 36.80	$ 34.50	$ 32.47	$ 30.67	$ 29.05	$ 27.60	$ 26.29	$ 25.09	$ 24.00	$ 23.00
$ 35.00	$ 46.67	$ 43.08	$ 40.00	$ 37.33	$ 35.00	$ 32.94	$ 31.11	$ 29.47	$ 28.00	$ 26.67	$ 25.45	$ 24.35	$ 23.33
$ 35.50	$ 47.33	$ 43.69	$ 40.57	$ 37.87	$ 35.50	$ 33.41	$ 31.56	$ 29.89	$ 28.40	$ 27.05	$ 25.82	$ 24.70	$ 23.67
$ 36.00	$ 48.00	$ 44.31	$ 41.14	$ 38.40	$ 36.00	$ 33.88	$ 32.00	$ 30.32	$ 28.80	$ 27.43	$ 26.18	$ 25.04	$ 24.00
$ 36.50	$ 48.67	$ 44.92	$ 41.71	$ 38.93	$ 36.50	$ 34.35	$ 32.44	$ 30.74	$ 29.20	$ 27.81	$ 26.55	$ 25.39	$ 24.33
$ 37.00	$ 49.33	$ 45.54	$ 42.29	$ 39.47	$ 37.00	$ 34.82	$ 32.89	$ 31.16	$ 29.60	$ 28.19	$ 26.91	$ 25.74	$ 24.67
$ 37.50	$ 50.00	$ 46.15	$ 42.86	$ 40.00	$ 37.50	$ 35.29	$ 33.33	$ 31.58	$ 30.00	$ 28.57	$ 27.27	$ 26.09	$ 25.00
$ 38.00	$ 50.67	$ 46.77	$ 43.43	$ 40.53	$ 38.00	$ 35.76	$ 33.78	$ 32.00	$ 30.40	$ 28.95	$ 27.64	$ 26.43	$ 25.33
$ 38.50	$ 51.33	$ 47.38	$ 44.00	$ 41.07	$ 38.50	$ 36.24	$ 34.22	$ 32.42	$ 30.80	$ 29.33	$ 28.00	$ 26.78	$ 25.67
$ 39.00	$ 52.00	$ 48.00	$ 44.57	$ 41.60	$ 39.00	$ 36.71	$ 34.67	$ 32.84	$ 31.20	$ 29.71	$ 28.36	$ 27.13	$ 26.00

Variable Hourly Pay Plan (VHP) with Earn-In-Period (EIP)

This is a well-accepted hourly pay plan that provides a nice focus on productivity. This pay plan changes hourly pay rates based on 6.25% productivity changes. The technician pay increase or decrease is between 3.2% and 5.6%. This provides a cushion for the technician during difficult times and a cushion for the house in better times.

Definition of VHP

VHP is the abbreviation for **Variable Hourly Pay**. In the VHP, the technician(s) are paid, by clock hour, at a rate that reflects their previous Earn-In-Period (EIP) production performance.

Definition of EIP

It is the abbreviation for **Earned-In-Period.** In an EIP Variable Rate Pay Plan, the technicians are paid by clock hour, based on their previous month's productivity. The EIP option reduces the manipulation of technicians slamming on the brakes and "banking" hours rather than flagging end-of-month jobs if they are not going to achieve the next level.

Establishing the EIP

Once the base production objectives on the pay grid have been quantified, the technician enters a 4 week **Earn-In-Period (EIP)**. The technician does not receive a different compensation amount for the hours worked during the period; they receive a new pay rate for hours produced in the next 4-week period and begin another Earn-In Period (EIP).

4-WEEK PERIOD	4-WEEK PERIOD	4-WEEK PERIOD

Initial Variable Hourly Pay (VHP)

Period 1 Earn-in-Period (EIP) ⟶ Period 1 Variable Hourly Pay (VHP)

Period 2 Earn-in-Period (EIP) ⟶ Period 2 Variable Hourly Pay (VHP)

Period 3 Earn-in-Period (EIP)

VHP Application to Hourly Positions

By using the Variable Hourly Pay Plan (VHP), we can increase the technician's hourly rate of pay while reducing the labor cost of sale.

The new pay rate is paid for every hour worked in the four weeks following the earn-in-period. The bonus rate is determined by the EIP/VHP Grid.

The grid illustrates the various cost-of-sale amounts for different hourly rates and production levels. As the technician's production increases, their cost-of-sale decreases.

As we consider the EIP/VHP in an hourly shop, the true cost of sales is not the dollar amount that you pay the technician; rather, it is the amount that you pay the technician over a period of time (day, week, etc.), divided by the number of hours billed or flagged.

Consider this example of an hourly quick-service technician prior to VHP:

Bill is paid $15.00 per clock hour. He works 8.0 hours per day.

Bill produces 4.6 hours of work during an average workday.

Bills pay is $15.00 x 8.0 = $120.00

$120.00 ÷ 4.6 (billed hours) = $26.09 true cost of sale.

In this current situation, Bill has no reason to do better.

The VHP method uses a grid that actually lowers the cost of sale as productivity increases, while increasing the technician hourly rate. See the chart below:

# of Flagged Hours	# of Hours Worked	Pay Rate	Productivity %	Effective Hourly Pay Rate (Pay Rate ÷ Productivity)		Suggested Daily Objective	Hourly Starting Pay Rate
23.0	40.0	$15.00	57.5%	$26.09		5.5	$15.00

	5.0 / 62.5%	5.5 / 68.8%	6.0 / 75.0%	6.5 / 81.3%	7.0 / 87.5%	7.5 / 93.8%	8.0 / 100.0%	8.5 / 106.3%	9.0 / 112.5%	9.5 / 118.8%	10.0 / 125.0%	10.5 / 131.3%	11.0 / 137.5%
$ 15.00	$ 24.00	$ 21.82	$ 20.00	$ 18.46	$ 17.14	$ 16.00	$ 15.00	$ 14.12	$ 13.33	$ 12.63	$ 12.00	$ 11.43	$ 10.91
$ 15.50	$ 24.80	$ 22.55	$ 20.67	$ 19.08	$ 17.71	$ 16.53	$ 15.50	$ 14.59	$ 13.78	$ 13.05	$ 12.40	$ 11.81	$ 11.27
$ 16.00	$ 25.60	$ 23.27	$ 21.33	$ 19.69	$ 18.29	$ 17.07	$ 16.00	$ 15.06	$ 14.22	$ 13.47	$ 12.80	$ 12.19	$ 11.64
$ 16.50	$ 26.40	$ 24.00	$ 22.00	$ 20.31	$ 18.86	$ 17.60	$ 16.50	$ 15.53	$ 14.67	$ 13.89	$ 13.20	$ 12.57	$ 12.00
$ 17.00	$ 27.20	$ 24.73	$ 22.67	$ 20.92	$ 19.43	$ 18.13	$ 17.00	$ 16.00	$ 15.11	$ 14.32	$ 13.60	$ 12.95	$ 12.36
$ 17.50	$ 28.00	$ 25.45	$ 23.33	$ 21.54	$ 20.00	$ 18.67	$ 17.50	$ 16.47	$ 15.56	$ 14.74	$ 14.00	$ 13.33	$ 12.73
$ 18.00	$ 28.80	$ 26.18	$ 24.00	$ 22.15	$ 20.57	$ 19.20	$ 18.00	$ 16.94	$ 16.00	$ 15.16	$ 14.40	$ 13.71	$ 13.09
$ 18.50	$ 29.60	$ 26.91	$ 24.67	$ 22.77	$ 21.14	$ 19.73	$ 18.50	$ 17.41	$ 16.44	$ 15.58	$ 14.80	$ 14.10	$ 13.45
$ 19.00	$ 30.40	$ 27.64	$ 25.33	$ 23.38	$ 21.71	$ 20.27	$ 19.00	$ 17.88	$ 16.89	$ 16.00	$ 15.20	$ 14.48	$ 13.82
$ 19.50	$ 31.20	$ 28.36	$ 26.00	$ 24.00	$ 22.29	$ 20.80	$ 19.50	$ 18.35	$ 17.33	$ 16.42	$ 15.60	$ 14.86	$ 14.18
$ 20.00	$ 32.00	$ 29.09	$ 26.67	$ 24.62	$ 22.86	$ 21.33	$ 20.00	$ 18.82	$ 17.78	$ 16.84	$ 16.00	$ 15.24	$ 14.55
$ 20.50	$ 32.80	$ 29.82	$ 27.33	$ 25.23	$ 23.43	$ 21.87	$ 20.50	$ 19.29	$ 18.22	$ 17.26	$ 16.40	$ 15.62	$ 14.91
$ 21.00	$ 33.60	$ 30.55	$ 28.00	$ 25.85	$ 24.00	$ 22.40	$ 21.00	$ 19.76	$ 18.67	$ 17.68	$ 16.80	$ 16.00	$ 15.27
$ 21.50	$ 34.40	$ 31.27	$ 28.67	$ 26.46	$ 24.57	$ 22.93	$ 21.50	$ 20.24	$ 19.11	$ 18.11	$ 17.20	$ 16.38	$ 15.64

In the new VHP pay plan, we will agree to pay Bill $15.50 per clock hour based on his willingness and commitment to produce an average of 5.5 flat rate or production hours per day. If Bill can accomplish an average of 6.0 or 6.5 hours per day during the EIP, he can increase his hourly compensation to $16.50 or $17.50, accordingly. In each of these events, the cost-of-sale is reduced, a win for all.

Changing technicians from flat rate to hourly using VHP/EIP.

Step 1 – Determine each technician's average production for the previous 10, 12, or 26-week period. This would be the same exercise that you perform when you implement production objectives. Use the grid to determine the starting hourly rate. For example:

Ralph is an A-Tech with an average productivity of 9.0 hours per day (112.5% productivity) as a Flat Rate Technician. His current flat-rate-pay rate is $28.00 per hour, and his cost-of-sale is $28.00 per hour. He works 8 hours per day and produces 9 hours, so his effective hourly pay rate is $31.50 per hour.

($28.00 X 9.0 hours = $252.00 ÷ 8.0 work hours = $31.50)

Under a typical hourly pay plan, productivity is likely to fall. The questions are: 1) How can we minimize the amount that it falls? 2) Will this reduction be worthwhile as we change the culture of our business?

During the production objective and implementation process, we should challenge Ralph to continue his current production of 9.0 hours per day. With his commitment, we will set this 9.0 hours as his daily objective.

As the grid indicates, as long as Ralph performs to objective, he will be paid $31.50 per hour, and the cost-of-sale will be $28.00. Nothing gained, nothing lost. Every 30 days, Ralph will exit an Earn-In-Period (EIP) and enter the next EIP. His hourly rate will adjust accordingly. It is recommended that the maximum monthly increase be 2 increases and 1-2 decreases. For example:

Ralph has a 112.5% (9.0 hours) objective. Based on his rate ($31.50), he is eligible to go up to $32.50 or $33.50 based on his EIP performance. Each of these levels will reduce his cost-of-sale. Or, if Ralph performs less than 112.5%, during the EIP, his rate could go down to $30.50 or $29.50 per hour. If Ralph moves up to an average of 125%+ (over multiple EIP's), his new rate would be $33.50 per hour and our cost-of-sale would be down to $26.80. When a technician hits the top tier for 2-EIP's in a row, consideration should be given to increasing his/her Production Objective. We must consider the work quality prior to making that decision.

This chart demonstrates the example of Ralph's one-month EIP potential with VHP. In this case, there is a $2.00 forward opportunity and a $2.00 backward opportunity.

	7.0 88%	7.5 94%	8.0 100%	8.5 106%	9.0 113%	9.5 119%	10.0 125%	10.5 131%	11.0 138%
$ 22.00	$ 25.14	$ 23.47	$ 22.00	$ 20.71	$ 19.56	$ 18.53	$ 17.60	$ 16.76	$ 16.00
$ 22.50	$ 25.71	$ 24.00	$ 22.50	$ 21.18	$ 20.00	$ 18.95	$ 18.00	$ 17.14	$ 16.36
$ 23.00	$ 26.29	$ 24.53	$ 23.00	$ 21.65	$ 20.44	$ 19.37	$ 18.40	$ 17.52	$ 16.73
$ 23.50	$ 26.86	$ 25.07	$ 23.50	$ 22.12	$ 20.89	$ 19.79	$ 18.80	$ 17.90	$ 17.09
$ 24.00	$ 27.43	$ 25.60	$ 24.00	$ 22.59	$ 21.33	$ 20.21	$ 19.20	$ 18.29	$ 17.45
$ 24.50	$ 28.00	$ 26.13	$ 24.50	$ 23.06	$ 21.78	$ 20.63	$ 19.60	$ 18.67	$ 17.82
$ 25.00	$ 28.57	$ 26.67	$ 25.00	$ 23.53	$ 22.22	$ 21.05	$ 20.00	$ 19.05	$ 18.18
$ 25.50	$ 29.14	$ 27.20	$ 25.50	$ 24.00	$ 22.67	$ 21.47	$ 20.40	$ 19.43	$ 18.55
$ 26.00	$ 29.71	$ 27.73	$ 26.00	$ 24.47	$ 23.11	$ 21.89	$ 20.80	$ 19.81	$ 18.91
$ 26.50	$ 30.29	$ 28.27	$ 26.50	$ 24.94	$ 23.56	$ 22.32	$ 21.20	$ 20.19	$ 19.27
$ 27.00	$ 30.86	$ 28.80	$ 27.00	$ 25.41	$ 24.00	$ 22.74	$ 21.60	$ 20.57	$ 19.64
$ 27.50	$ 31.43	$ 29.33	$ 27.50	$ 25.88	$ 24.44	$ 23.16	$ 22.00	$ 20.95	$ 20.00
$ 28.00	$ 32.00	$ 29.87	$ 28.00	$ 26.35	$ 24.89	$ 23.58	$ 22.40	$ 21.33	$ 20.36
$ 28.50	$ 32.57	$ 30.40	$ 28.50	$ 26.82	$ 25.33	$ 24.00	$ 22.80	$ 21.71	$ 20.73
$ 29.00	$ 33.14	$ 30.93	$ 29.00	$ 27.29	$ 25.78	$ 24.42	$ 23.20	$ 22.10	$ 21.09
$ 29.50	$ 33.71	$ 31.47	$ 29.50	$ 27.76	$ 26.22	$ 24.84	$ 23.60	$ 22.48	$ 21.45
$ 30.00	$ 34.29	$ 32.00	$ 30.00	$ 28.24	$ 26.67	$ 25.26	$ 24.00	$ 22.86	$ 21.82
$ 30.50	$ 34.86	$ 32.53	$ 30.50	$ 28.71	$ 27.11	$ 25.68	$ 24.40	$ 23.24	$ 22.18
$ 31.00	$ 35.43	$ 33.07	$ 31.00	$ 29.18	$ 27.56	$ 26.11	$ 24.80	$ 23.62	$ 22.55
$ 31.50	$ 36.00	$ 33.60	$ 31.50	$ 29.65	$ 28.00	$ 26.53	$ 25.20	$ 24.00	$ 22.91
$ 32.00	$ 36.57	$ 34.13	$ 32.00	$ 30.12	$ 28.44	$ 26.95	$ 25.60	$ 24.38	$ 23.27
$ 32.50	$ 37.14	$ 34.67	$ 32.50	$ 30.59	$ 28.89	$ 27.37	$ 26.00	$ 24.76	$ 23.64
$ 33.00	$ 37.71	$ 35.20	$ 33.00	$ 31.06	$ 29.33	$ 27.79	$ 26.40	$ 25.14	$ 24.00
$ 33.50	$ 38.29	$ 35.73	$ 33.50	$ 31.53	$ 29.78	$ 28.21	$ 26.80	$ 25.52	$ 24.36
$ 34.00	$ 38.86	$ 36.27	$ 34.00	$ 32.00	$ 30.22	$ 28.63	$ 27.20	$ 25.90	$ 24.73
$ 34.50	$ 39.43	$ 36.80	$ 34.50	$ 32.47	$ 30.67	$ 29.05	$ 27.60	$ 26.29	$ 25.09

COST OF SALE

(Row labels at left, read top to bottom: HOURLY PAY RATE)

This pay plan can be annoying to your payroll department, but in an hourly shop, any pay plan is going to be annoying. The best way to do this is to cost the technicians at their Base Objective Rate and make monthly reconciliations, which they should be doing anyway.

When using a clock-hour pay plan, it is important to understand the overtime laws of your state. In addition, most dealerships that use hourly pay plans limit their technicians to 40 hours.

Hourly Pay Plan – Lateral Support

This pay plan is simply paying your technicians an hourly rate. The lateral support structure seems to be the most effective method of managing technician behavior. Without intervention to monitor production, it is not unusual to see a 20-30% reduction in productivity. As we look back at the example of an assembly line, imagine if there were no investigation or counseling when the line stopped. Or what if the line didn't stop? What would the end product look like?

If and when we consider changing technicians to an hourly pay plan, here are some tips to help reduce lost productivity:

1. Operate in Lateral Support Groups. You may choose to use the options of "dispatch within the structure", mentioned earlier in this chapter. For many years, studies have determined that the best employee-to-manager ratio is 4:1 or 5:1. In this situation, the Group Leader should become a part of service management.

2. Develop an hourly pay plan for Group Leader. Prepare a job description or process document outlining the role of the Group Leader:

   - Dispatching responsibilities:
     1) skill match; 2) customer status or completion time; 3) individual technician production objectives

   - Determine hourly pay rate with Group Leader, consider previous productivity (-10% if currently on flat rate), calculate upwards for positive changes that can be made for improving productivity.

   - Develop Group Leader Bonus based on each of the group technicians that meet or exceed their production objective for the pay period. This bonus should be an expense and based on your budget but, consider it to be a vital part of maintaining your productivity. An example might be $100 bonus for each technician that meets or exceeds their objective for a 2-week pay period.

3. With the Group Leader at your side, determine the base objective for each technician (typically current production – 10%).

- Determine hourly pay rate for each technician, consider previous productivity (-10% if currently on flat rate)

- The add-back will be the amount of improvement that the technician commits to, after the 10% reduction. This new number will be the technician's objective, and the number that the Group Leader's bonus is calculated.

In the example below, the technician is currently paid $25.00 per flat-rate-hour. This technician is 105% productive (flags 8.4 hours in an 8.0-hour workday). The hourly base rate is $26.25 per hour. Because it is appropriate to expect that productivity will decline, you may decide to implement a 10% setback (the tech that currently produces 8.4 hours will, if you are lucky, produce 7.6 hours).

Current Flat Rate Hourly Pay		Current Productivity %		Base Pay		10% Setback		Objective Add-Back %		New Hourly Pay-Rate
$25.00	X	105%	=	$26.25	-	$2.63	+	5%	=	$24.88

1. Meet with each technician and the group leader to discuss their previous performance and the roadblocks that cause them to perform at the current level.

- Explain the setback with each technician and agree on an hourly rate, in agreement for a production objective agreement.

A conversation might go something like this (refer to the previous calculation):

"Hello Jimmy. If you are agreeable, we are going to change you to from flat rate to hourly pay."

"You will be in a lateral support group with Bob as your group leader. Are you good with that?"

(Please see Note 1.)

"As Bob and I work on your hourly rate calculation, we need to discuss a few things with you."

"First of all, you have averaged about 8.4 hours per day in production. At $25.00 per hour, that means that your true hourly rate is $26.25. The challenge is that when we convert to hourly, the typical setback is more than 10%. So, if I calculate a 10% setback, your rate will be $23.62, and your daily objective will be 7.6 hours-per-day."

"My question to you is, could you produce more hours? If so, what are the challenges?"

Listen to the challenges and discuss the options:

1. "I will fix this. Here is how..."

2. "I will research this, and we can revisit."

3. "I am sorry, but I have no control over that."

"As a result, how many additional hours do you believe you could add back because of these changes?"

As the graph shows, this would be an add-back and could be used to determine the overall hourly pay rate for the technician. The 5% add-back would take the technicians hourly rate to $24.88, which is very comparable to their current situation. If the technician can convince you and their group leader that they can perform at a higher level, you could adjust the add-back accordingly.

- Once this new process is implemented, it will be the Group Leader's responsibility to ensure that the technicians accomplish their objectives.

Note 1: "With and for". Prior to assigning technicians to groups, each technician should be allowed to voice input as to whom they would like to work with.

A clock hour pay plan will almost always result in a reduction in productivity compared to a flat-rate-pay plan. Even so, it may make perfect sense to do this. Will it improve your ability to hire and retain technicians? If so, it might be a good idea. In some markets, flat-rate pay plans just aren't accepted. By utilizing the implementation described above, you should minimize the reduction.

When using a clock-hour pay plan, it is important to understand the overtime laws of your state. In addition, most dealerships that use hourly pay plans limit their technicians to 40 hours.

CONCLUSION

From the horse, to the bull, to the starfish, the story is told. In my five decades in the automobile industry, I have had a great deal of success, but I always considered myself to be a student of the business. I always wanted to learn more, and I was fortunate to be in situations that supported my appetite for this.

This book is a collection of processes, theories, and concepts that I have encountered on this journey of firsthand experience and the thousand or so managers with whom I have interacted.

"With knowledge comes strength." These ideas, processes, and concepts are being used successfully in dealerships.

Please consider these tips as you decide to implement any of these processes:

- Involve your team - find out what is most important to them. Many times, these are the same things that are important to you. So now it is their idea. This creates buy-in. When I hear a majority of concerns about dispatch fairness, it opens my eyes to the idea of changing the structure. Act "with and for" your team, not against.

- Focus on your inventory – What is your inventory? Hours! We all love gross profit, but gross profit does not happen until we sell some of our inventory. When this becomes the key focus in your organization, your team will begin recognizing the areas of waste (technician utilization). I've never met a sales manager, or dealer for that matter, who didnt know how many cars and trucks they sold yesterday. But I have met many, many service managers, directors and dealers that don't know how many hours they sold yesterday.

- Create a process document or playbook for every process or change that you implement. In today's world, top performing dealerships have been successful in implementing variants of structures and pay plans to provide adaptability. For example, in one study, 16% of technicians indicated that they love flat rate. So, even if you make a major change in pay structure, should flat rate be an option? Without a process document or playbook, it could appear that your shop is a free-for-all.

- Process for managing the process – The most frequent mistake that I have seen is that a shop implements Production Objectives correctly. They do a great job of daily objective management (morning huddles, etc.). A year later, I get a call. Productivity was rocking along, setting records, but for the last couple of months, we're sliding backward. My first question: "Tell me about your morning huddles." The response hovers right around 100%: "We kinda stopped doing them. Things were going so well." Bingo! This is where the service department got struck by Satan's horrible curse called "Complacency"!

Use the logic of "Structured Technique" and "Operational Technique" to define how this process will be governed. Your structured technique might assign the meetings to the group leaders, dispatcher, or shop foreman. Your operational technique is how you verify that the process is adhered to. Perhaps the group leader, dispatcher, or shop fore-man signs off on the daily meeting sheet and turns it in to you. Maybe you visit one of the meetings each morning. You should be asking questions when a technician misses their objective for two of more days.

- When in doubt, get help. There are plenty of consulting companies (including the author of this book) that can assist in the design and implementation of any of these concepts. Do not shortcut the steps involved in the proper implementation of these processes.

Wishing you the strength and wisdom to become a superstar and a pioneer for positive change in a very challenging industry. Amen.

NOTE: Most of the documents displayed and discussed in this book are available for download, at no charge, in PDF format at **www.fixedopshelp.com.**

ABOUT THE AUTHOR

Charlie Waters has enjoyed a five-decade career in the dealership fixed operations business.

As a child, Waters had a passion for understanding mechanical devices, especially cars. At 9 years old, he received discipline for completely disassembling the family's lawn mower engine, just to see how it worked. Because the mower started up and ran when he reassembled it, his "sentence" was reduced!

He began his dealership career as a technician and quickly accelerated through every service department role to Assistant Service Manager within eight years. During the following 27 years, he served as Service Manager, Director, and Fixed Ops Director for three different large dealerships and a group of ten dealerships.

Waters has spent over 15 years as a Fixed Operations trainer and consultant, including the last several years as a business owner. His business, Fixed Ops Resource, is a reliable source for virtual training and information, such as that found in this book. He is very familiar with the methods and theories discussed in this book and has actually implemented and used most of them. As a trainer/consultant, Waters has worked with manufacturers including General Motors, Ford, VW and Harley Davidson in the development and delivery of training to Parts, Service and Body Shop Managers.

Waters has accomplished a great deal of success as a result of his continued passion to be a student of this business, always looking for better best practices. He understands accounting, financial statements, procedures, and processes that lead to improvements.

In addition to his fixed operations skills, Waters is also:

- A former Pacific Institute facilitator in cognitive psychology training.

- A DiSC behavior profile facilitator

- A Predictive Index (PI) profile facilitator.

- A past Rotary Club president.

Waters, his wife, Christina, and daughter, Maezie, reside in Jacksonville, Florida.

ACKNOWLEDGEMENTS

I have been fortunate not only to learn from some of the finest mentors in this field but also to have had opportunities presented to me at pivotal moments. Two decades ago, I envisioned a future where I would sit on a front porch swing, reflecting on the legacy I hoped to have had a positive impact on others. While I may not possess a swing or even a front porch, I am deeply convinced that I have indeed touched the lives of many, just as so many have touched mine.

I wrote this book to make a difference in the lives of additional people. I owe my personal success and wisdom to the following folks:

- Carl Farris - RIP. Carl, my high school auto shop instructor. You were my first mentor and inspiration in this business. You were so creative, which I admired and have tried to replicate. It was awesome to reunite with you years after high school. Thank you for your mentorship. I am blessed to have had you in my life.

- Joe Key - Thank you, Joe, for believing in me, even when others didn't. Your friendship is great, and your mentorship was always special, even when we didn't agree. You taught me that it was okay not to agree, to challenge the norm, and to find common ground. A great lesson. In addition, you taught me the concept that I respect the most: "If it ain't in writing, it never happened!"

- Mike Shad - Thank you for leading and mentoring me and many others in culture when culture was not a popular term. Your philosophy of honesty and integrity has been burned into the soul of myself and others. That is special!

- Greg Thrasher - aka "Cool Breeze" – You introduced me to many of these concept's 30+ years ago. We remain friends to this day. I always knew that you were a cool breeze, but I only found out recently that this was your nickname. Thank you, my friend.

- David Green – Thanks for being that Service Manager that I relied on in the Introduction. You instructed me to pick-up-the-legal-pad and make a list. That was the advice that was needed at the time. David has always been a friend and a mentor.

- Ed Roberts (aka JR) – July 20, 1992, was a great day. Watching you grow over the years has been an amazing experience. You were the "Starfish" on the beach that made every bit of effort worthwhile. Thank you for what you have done to improve this business. Thank you for being a mentor to me, especially for giving me the encouragement to complete this book.

- Barry Keene (aka JK) – It has been a blast to watch you grow into one of the finest Fixed Operations Directors in the country. Your approach to creating teamwork and a great culture is amazing. You truly have a servant's heart. I miss you calling me to ask, "How do I calculate ELR to get a certain gross profit?" I guess it finally stuck! Congratulations on your success.

- Richard Jordan – While you are a crossbreed, having worked under the culture of multiple dealer groups, you have been an awesome friend and mentor. The stories that you tell are not only funny, but also loaded with information to help change and improve the business. Thank you, my friend.

- Duane Curto – You cannot imagine my appreciation for the assistance that you have provided in helping me get this book over the curb. It is something that I thought I would never do. Your input has been awesome.

Others – Many additional people have been mentors and influencers in my journey as a student of this business. These people have all assisted me in understanding and implementing the policies, processes, and procedures discussed in this book. These people include, but are not limited to:

- Quentin Jones

- Terry Carlisle

- George Goldberg

- Chuck Wenzler

- Greg Lingenfelder

- Rick Yanac

- The hundreds of parts, service and body shop managers that I've had the pleasure of training. I learn from your feedback and experiences.

INDEX

To download free PDF Index to this book, please go to **www.fixedopshelp.com**

This Index tool will assist you in using this book as a reference guide in the future.